The Art of the Seductress

Also By Arthur Asa Berger
Li'l Abner,
The Evangelical Hamburger
Pop Culture
About Man
The Comic Stripped American
The TV-Guided American
Film in SOCIETY
Television as an Instrument of Terror
Media Analysis Techniques
Signs in Contemporary Culture
Television in SOCIETY
Semiotics of Advertising
Media USA
Seeing is Believing: An Introduction to Visual Communication
Political Culture and Public Opinion
Agitpop: Political Culture and Communication Theory
Scripts: Writing for Radio and Television
Media Research Techniques
Reading Matter
Popular Culture Genres
An Anatomy of Humor
Improving Writing Skills
Blind Men & Elephants: Perspectives on Humor
Cultural Criticism: A Primer of Key Concepts
Essentials of Mass Communication Theory
Manufacturing Desire: Media, Popular Culture & Everyday Life
Narratives in Popular Culture, Media & Everyday Life
The Genius of the Jewish Joke
Bloom's Morning
The Art of Comedy Writing
Postmortem for a Postmodernist
The Postmodern Presence
Die Laughing
Murder Ad Nauseam
Media & Communication Research Methods
Ads, Fads & Consumer Culture
Jewish Jesters
Video Games: A Popular Culture Phenomenon
The Agent in the Agency: Media, Popular Culture, Everyday Life
The Mass Comm Murders: Five Media Theorists Self-Destruct

The Art of the Seductress

Techniques of the Great Seductresses
from Biblical Times to the Postmodern Era

Arthur Asa Berger

Writers Club Press
San Jose New York Lincoln Shanghai

The Art of the Seductress
Techniques of the Great Seductresses
from Biblical Times to the Postmodern Era

Writers Club Press
an imprint of iUniverse, Inc.

For information address:
iUniverse, Inc.
5220 S. 16th St., Suite 200
Lincoln, NE 68512
www.iuniverse.com

ISBN: 0-595-23077-6

Printed in the United States of America

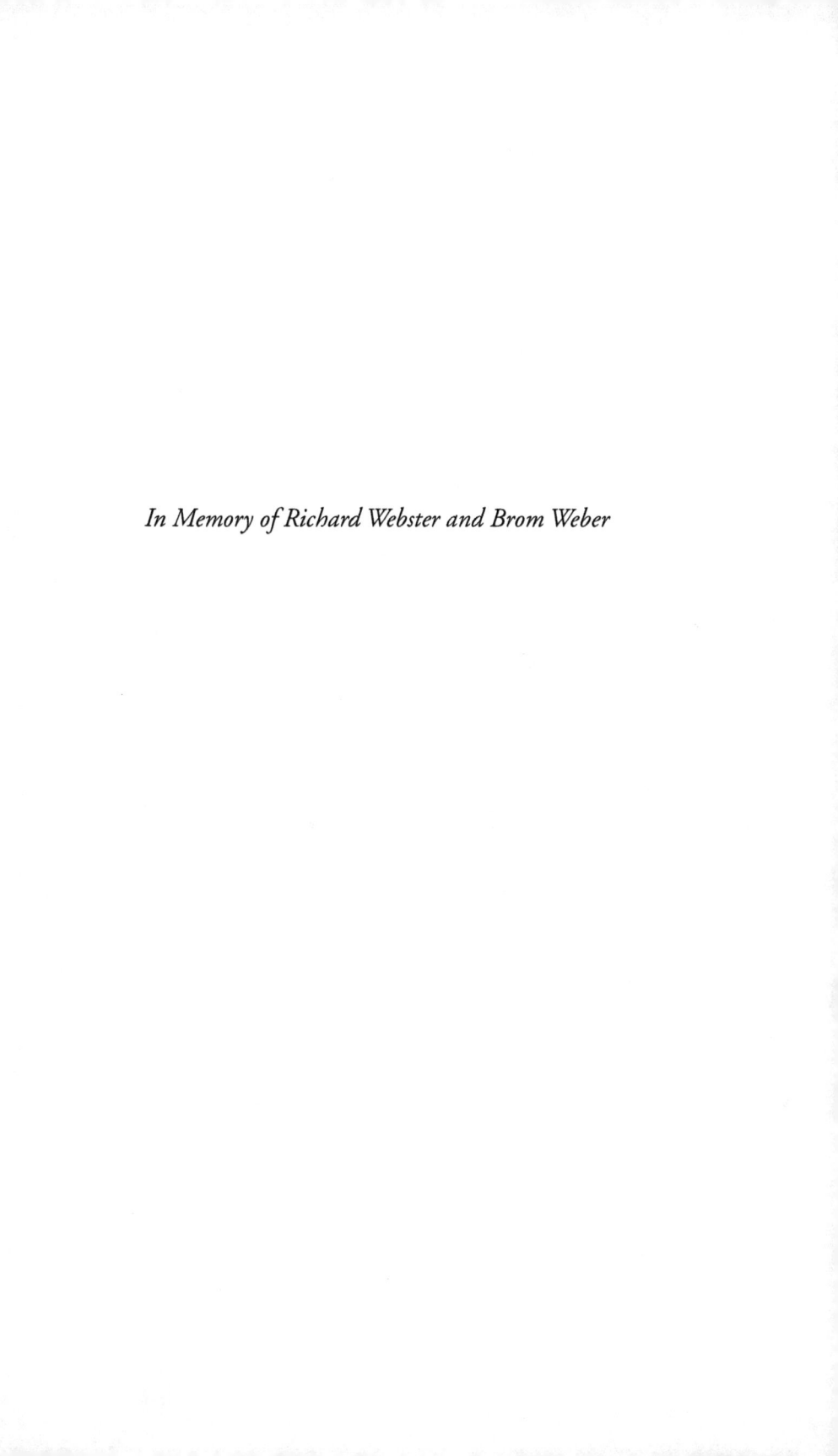

In Memory of Richard Webster and Brom Weber

Omnia vincit Amor: et nos cedamus Amori

CONTENTS

PREFACE: A NOTE FROM A THEORETICAL SCHOLAR OF SEDUCTRESSES

Little did I know, when I embarked on this study of the techniques used by the great seductresses, where it would lead me or what I would learn. I am, I should point out, a *theoretical* scholar of the seductress. My wife informed me that under no circumstances, despite my desire to learn as much as I could about seductresses, would I be permitted to do field research. It would be far too dangerous to my well being on any number of fronts, she suggested. And with good reason, for the seductress, as you will see when you read this book, is a powerful and, in many cases, a dangerous woman.

I have found seductresses in The Bible, in myth, in folklore, in literature, and in history. But it's been very difficult to find works that show, in any significant detail, seductresses in action. Thus, it has been quite difficult to discover material on the *techniques* used by seductresses in works of fiction or books that showed the way famous real-life seductresses work.

(In many cases, seductresses may be working their wiles but men are not aware or conscious of the fact that they are being seduced. Thus, let me suggest that the only realistic answer a man can give to the question "have you ever been seduced by a woman?" is "not as far as *I* know!")

The Art of Seduction: A User's Manual

There are many "how-to" books—which profess to teach women how to be successful seductresses. But my desire was not to write a manual on how to be a seductress but rather to consider the *techniques* of the seductress from a historical perspective—to examine some of our most celebrated and interesting seductresses—what we might call "super-star seductresses."

I hope you will find this book interesting and edifying. Some women who wish to develop their abilities as seductresses might find this inquiry instructive, since I spell out, in considerable detail, how seductresses have charmed men over the millennia. In a sense, then, this book can be considered "A User's Manual." But other women might wish to give the book to their boyfriends or husbands to scare the hell out of them, since in most cases, the consequences of consorting with a seductress are disastrous, to put it mildly. Bill Clinton is only the latest example of someone important who has paid a great price for being tempted by a seductress.

ACKNOWLEDGMENTS

I'd like to thank all the historians, Biblical scholars, anthropologists, psychologists and others, whose research into the lives of various seductresses has made this book possible. I also owe a debt of gratitude to all the seductresses whose exploits and whose techniques I have discussed.

CHAPTER 1

SEDUCTIO AD ABSURDUM

This little book deals with one rather specialized aspect of the so-called "battle of the sexes"…an historical study of the techniques of seduction used by women who seduce men. It also deals with seduction techniques in different cultures and societies. At times I take a somewhat latitudinarian view of seduction and consider it to include temptation and other matters like it that do not necessarily end up in sexual intercourse or some other kind of a sexual relationship. But for the most part, I equate seduction with a sexual relationship.

You will learn about the techniques used by some of the most famous and infamous seductresses such as Eve, Lilith, Judith, Cleopatra, Messalina, Theodora, Catherine the Great, Madame de Pompadour and Charlotte Manning, the temptress in Mickey Spillane's murder mystery, *I The Jury*. And you will learn what happens to men who become "ensnared" by seductresses.

Just after I started on this book I attended a dinner party which had a number of women in their late eighties (and some who were only a decade or two younger). I mentioned that I was writing a book on seduction techniques used by women and the women at the dinner party had a wonderful time suggesting novels, Biblical characters, and myths for me to consider. I was astounded at how interested they were in the subject and how easily these eighty-five year old ladies talked about seduction. They giggled and laughed a lot, too, suggesting a certain amount of unconscious anxiety about the subject.

Seduction and The Battle of the Sexes

To return to my military metaphor, in the "war between the sexes," seduction has been likened to a battle, a momentary engagement with "the enemy." This battle has one major purpose most of the time…sexual pleasure, of one sort or another. Usually sexual intercourse but in our postmodern post-Clintonian era, other forms of temptation and other sexual practices will be accepted. In my study of seductresses, let me point out, I will also deal with several women who tempt men and seduce them for reasons other than sexual desire.

There's something interesting about the word "seduction" When we hear the term we often think of it in terms of men seducing women. This is because most of the time it is men who seduce women. Women may be temptresses and teases, but in the popular imagination men are the real seducers. As this book demonstrates, however, women also have done their fair share of seducing. That explains why the seductress is one of the archetypes of myth, folklore and literature.

When men look at beautiful women, fantasies of seduction often pop into their minds. Men may get sexual satisfaction from their wives but quite often they don't get the satisfaction of their *erotic* fantasies from them. The same, of course, applies to women. Men seldom think about the fact that women may also harbor fantasies of seduction when they see men they deem desirable.

One reason men make this error is that they tend to see women, or perhaps it is more accurate to say that they want to see women as essentially innocent and weak. Sexy, yes. Alluring, yes. But essentially, and by nature, passive.

Probably this is because, until the last few decades or so, only women's bodies were seen as legitimate objects of lust and desire. Women's bodies still dominate the magazine covers in most countries. We see a good deal more breast and cleavage and midriff and bellybutton displays nowadays, and articles on sexual techniques that in years past would never be listed on covers or even dealt with. There are articles, almost clinical in nature, about facilitating orgasms and various arcane sexual practices.

In recent years, however, our attitudes have changed, and men's bodies…selling underwear and other items…now have become objects of feminine lust and desire. But generally speaking, we still don't see revealing photos of men's bodies on magazine covers.

Seduction in the Dictionary

The term "seduction" is defined in dictionaries as "being led astray." *Seductio* in Latin means "lead astray." But what does "led astray" mean? Very little, I would say. And who is leading whom astray? When thinking about seductresses we might ask a number of pertinent questions, for which I have supplied answers:

who?	a woman
is doing what?	is seducing
to whom?	a man (but not always)
using what techniques?	touch, smell, words, etc.
when?	time of seduction
where?	place of seduction
for how long?	the time the seduction takes
for what reasons?	sexual gratification?
with what consequences?	pleasure? security? power?

All of this is quite abstract and seems relatively simple. That's because the dictionary definition oversimplifies matters. If you look at a thesaurus, however, under the term seduction you find many terms dealing with a number of different aspects of seduction, which show how complicated it is. I will deal with some of these categories and say something about what the terms in each category suggest.

Unchastity. One set of terms, under the general category of "unchastity," has words such as betrayal, violation, defloration, debauchment, and despoilment. These terms suggest a male seducer and female "victim" who is debauched, deflowered or violated. This is because we use the term chaste for women and not for men, so seduction often involves a woman being despoiled…a process that is not, so the thesaurus suggests, a happy one.

This perspective is very old-fashioned. Many teenage girls in America and elsewhere, no doubt, see losing their virginity as highly desirable and they often aren't too choosy about who they select to deflower them. Sex, for these teenagers, is about as romantic as eating popcorn and there's almost a game-like aspect to being deflowered: young girls, according to some newspaper articles I've read, sometimes compete to see who can become deflowered first!

Love. Under the category of "love," however, we find different synonyms: endear, charm, infatuate, fascinate, attract, allure, captivate, bewitch, carry away, sweep off one's feet, vamp, tempt and tantalize. These words suggest a female seductress and a male who is seduced. Here the dangerous aspects of female sexuality are hinted at…women have the ability to make men lose their rationality, to succumb to temptation, or be carried away by emotions.

Seduction, as dealt with in the thesaurus, is considerably different from male sexual lust. In the Bible, there are many instances in which a man sees a woman and desires her, sends for her, and almost immediately has sex with her. There is no suggestion of seductiveness on the part of the woman, only that her beauty led to her being desired by a powerful male.

Allurement. The category "allurement" has other synonyms of interest. It lists verbs such as allure, entice, inveigle, give the come-on or bat the eyes at, flirt, coax, ensnare, bait the hook, and so on. Here we find seduction described as a matter of becoming ensnared (as in a net) or hooked (like a fish). For nouns we have allurement, enticement, temptation, tantalization, seduction, beguilement, captivation, snaring, enchantment, enthrallment, bewitchment, glamour, appeal, magnetism, charisma, song of the Sirens, voice of the tempter, forbidden fruit.

The adjectives connected to allurement are similar. We find words such as fascinating, captivating, charming, enchanting, spellbinding, enravishing, bewitching, beguiling, seducing, tantalizing, irresistible, hypnotic, sirenic, tempting, and exciting. There is a sense, here, that there's something magical about women's powers to put a spell on men, to hypnotize them, to tempt them (recalling the story of Adam and Eve in the Garden), and in the case of the Sirens in *The Odyssey*, to lure them to their destruction. Seduction, it is implied, is something women do! And the consequences for men are terrible.

As Bram Dijkstra points out in his book *Evil Sisters,* a study of vamps and similar types of women: Even today Hollywood and popular culture are overrun by "vamps." As a verb, "to vamp" came to be used to describe the sundry predatory activities of man-hungry women, and the phrase "Kiss me, my fool!"...with which Theda [Bara] dispatched her victims...became a favorite line in the repertoire of several generations of pop-culture wits.

Dijkstra discusses the novel *A Fool There Was* by Porter Edward Browne, which was based on his famous play:

> In Browne's original those words were almost as heavily weighted with ideology and politics as the Vampire's final kiss itself. Her arrogant order was a witch's incantation permitting the feminine principle to call up whatever degenerative, self-destructive impulses still remained with the evolutionary male. (*Evil Sisters*, page 28)

There is something thought to be in the very nature of men, Dykstra suggests, that enables these seductresses to work their magic. (For those who are interested in the subject, I will discuss the role of the senses in seduction and sexual relations in the Appendix.)

Dijkstra offers an example from *A Fool There Was* that describes the hypnotic power of these "evil women":

"His eyes were upon her. She made no movement. She paused not in her indolent sinuous walk. Her eyes were upon him; and that was all…dark eyes, glowing, inscrutable, beautiful with the beauty that was hers. And his eyes were on her." (*Evil Sisters*, p. 38)

We see that the beauty and power of these women to mesmerize men was one of the sources of their power. But there are other powers that seductresses have…namely the power of their voices, as the example of the Sirens in Homer's *The Odyssey* suggests.

The Sirens: A Case Study

The Sirens, in mythology, sang to seafarers who were so spellbound by their voices that they were lured to waters where their boats broke up. Homer has Circe describe the Sirens to Odysseus in *the Odyssey*. She tells him about the dangers he will face as he makes his way back to Greece:

> …Your next encounter will be with the Sirens, who bewitch everybody that approaches them. There is no home-coming forthe man who draws near them unawares and hears the Sirens' voices; no welcome from his wife, no little children brightening at their father's return. For with the music of their song the Sirens cast their spell upon him, as they sit there in a meadow piled high with the mouldering skeletons of men, whose withered skin still hangs upon their bones.

She tells Odysseus to put wax in his men's ears so they can't hear the sirens and that if he wishes to hear them, to have his men tie him to the mast so he can't escape and not release him.

> Later, he tells us what it was like to hear the Sirens: The lovely voices came to me across the water, and my heart was filled with such a longing to listen that with nod and frown I signed to my men to set me free. But they swung forward to their oars and rowed ahead.

Thus Ulysses was able to hear the enchanting voices of the Sirens but escape being lured to his destruction by them.

There are, then, many different ways of looking at the term seduction or, to be more precise, many different aspects of seduction. In some cases, when we are dealing with male seducers, innocent women are portrayed as victims of unscrupulous debauchers and in other cases, when we are dealing with seductresses, men are powerless to resist the charms and bewitching powers of predatory women.

Seduction and Male Resistance

This book is different from many books dealing with sexuality and seduction in that it offers a historical perspective on the various techniques women have used to seduce men over the past few thousand years. It is, then, a book that deals with cultural practices and historical developments, and is not, in essence, a "how-to" methodology book (though, of course, it can be used as such). It is an examination of some of our greatest, most successful seductresses in fiction, in myth and folklore, and in real life.

Let me turn to one important implication of the term seduction. When we think of seductresses one thing that we have to consider is the matter of male resistance. If there is no resistance, if a man enters into a sexual relationship without *having to be* "led astray," we do not, as I see things, really have seduction. We have consensual sex. Seduction by a woman ultimately ends up as sex between willing partners but also, as we will understand the term, it involves overcoming resistance.

Why might a man "resist" having sex with a woman? There could be any number of reasons, some of which I will list below:

1. he might find the woman trying to seduce him unattractive,
2. he might be married and be afraid of getting involved in something messy and even dangerous,

3. he might be young and the seductress might be a much older woman, whom he does not find desirable (like the Maid of Bath)

4. he might be in love with someone else,

5. he might be deeply religious, and have ethical problems about having a sexual relationship with someone he is not married to,

6. he may be scared of women,

7. he might feel that his masculinity is under attack in that conventionally it is the males who are supposed to be assertive,

8. he might be afraid of getting caught and suffering shame, humiliation, and financial damage.

9. he may be afraid of getting sexually transmitted diseases,

10. he might have "performance anxiety" about the sex act and be afraid of not being able to "satisfy" his seductress,

11. he may be sexually disfunctional and incapable of having sexual intercourse with a woman, and

12. he may need (but have forgotten) his Viagra.

Is it not curious that we are not terribly surprised when an older man marries a much younger woman but we raise our eyebrows when an older woman marries a much younger man? In many cases we describe the older man as having married what we call a "trophy" wife…a symbol of his wealth and power. Power has been described, we must remember, as the ultimate aphrodisiac! But what about the woman who marries a much younger man? We generally assume it can *only* be because the younger man is doing so for financial gain. This view is both sexist and ageist!

In a sense, then, feminine seduction involves the power to overcome resistance and the ability to use a woman's sexuality to dominate some male. It involves a reversal of the usual situation in which men see women they desire, lust after them, and if necessary, attempt to seduce them. Feminine seduction involves…among other things…a triumph of intelligence, imagination, and guile over psychological resistance and physical power. Men are, after all, physically stronger than women…with rare exceptions.

So in many cases women have to convince men that having sex with them is really what they had in mind, even though they might not have been conscious of this desire. This raises an interesting question. Can there be an *irony* of seduction? Is it possible that many men who think they are seducing a woman are, in fact, being seduced themselves? That is, many men may have the illusions that *they* are the seducer when in fact they are the seducee? In how many cases is it not the fact that the hunter is, in actuality, the hunted?

This book, then, in addition to be a book about one aspect of female sexuality can also function as an expose and help men become more realistic about themselves and their relations with women. Seduction is, it turns out, a complex matter…involving visual images, smell, touch, taste, time, national character, and personality.

The Complexity of Seduction

Sexual intercourse is, at the simplest level, a physical activity. It is, ideally speaking, the culmination of a process of foreplay and love making. There are numerous positions that can be used by people having sex, but in the final analysis, it all adds up to the same thing: one way or another a male penetrates a female.

But seduction…which also generally leads to sexual intercourse…is an incredibly complex phenomenon. For example, we might consider whether there are variations in seduction techniques based on nationalities? Thus, there may be a French style of seduction, an Italian style of seduction, a German style of seduction, an English style of seduction, a Japanese style of seduction, an American style of seduction, and so on, ad infinitum.

There is also, as I suggested above, the relationship that exists between smell and seduction, taste and seduction, social class and seduction, race and seduction, age and seduction, religion and seduction, climate and seduction, intelligence and seduction, political ideology and

seduction...in short, almost everything conceivable (including concep-
tion) relates to seduction one way or another. I will deal with a number of
these matters in this book. But do these aspects of seduction lead to different *kinds* of seduction? I consider this question in the following discus-
sions of the dangers of seductresses, from Proverbs, and of the techniques
of the seductress, from Ovid.

The Seductress in Proverbs 7

One of the most important cautionary tales in the Bible...of which, as
we have seen, there are many...comes in Proverbs 7. In Proverbs there are
earlier warnings, such as in Proverbs 2 on the "Moral Benefits of Wisdom"
which has a passage about the benefits of wisdom:

> It will save you also from the adulteress from the wayward wife
> with her seductive words who has left the partner of her youth
> and ignored the covenant she made before god. For her house
> leads down to death...

And there is another caution in Proverbs 5, which is a "Warning
Against Adultery." In Proverbs 5 we read:

> For the lips of an adulteress drip with honey and her speech is
> smoother than oil; but in the end she is bitter as gall, sharp as a
> double-edged sword. Her feet go down to death;

These two passages both deal with seduction and both show that seductresses destroy men.

We have to be careful because although adulteresses (which I take to
refer to seductresses, in general, whether or not they are married) seduce us
with lips that "drip honey" and with speech "smoother than oil," consorting with them leads to death. "None who go to her return or attain the
paths of life" we are told. We can resist them if we have wisdom or we take
heed of the warnings given to us about them. It is because we take heed of

the warnings that are given to us or have developed a moral sensibility that we are able to resist such women…their honeyed lips, their smooth speech.

But it is in Proverbs 7, "Warning Against the Adulteress" that we find the most explicit and most elaborated examination of the way seductresses work. I will quote Proverbs 7 in its entirety so we can discuss the techniques they use in some detail.

Proverbs 7: "Warning Against the Adulteress"

My son, keep my words and store up my commands within you.

Keep my commands and you will live; guard my teachings as the apple of your eye. Bind them on your fingers; write them on the table of your heart. Say to wisdom, "You are my sister," and call understanding your kinsman; they will keep you from the adulteress, from the wayward wife with her seductive words. At the window of my house I looked out through the lattice.

I saw among the simple, I noticed among the young men, a youth who lacked judgment. He was going down the street near her corner, walking along in the direction of her house at twilight, as the day was fading, as the dark of night set in. Then out came a woman to meet him, dressed like a prostitute and with crafty intent. (She is loud and defiant, her feet never stay at home; now in the street, now in the squares, at every corner she lurks.) She took hold of him and kissed him and with a brazen face she said: "I have fellowship offerings at home; today I fulfilled my vows. So I came out to meet you; I looked for you and have found you! I have covered my bed with colored linens from Egypt. I have perfumed my bed with myrrh, aloes and cinnamon. Come, let's drink deep of love till morning; let's enjoy ourselves with love! My husband is not at home; he has gone on a long journey. He took his purse filled with money and will not be home till full moon." With persuasive words she led him astray; she seduced him with her smooth talk. All at one he followed her like an ox going to the slaughter, like a deer stepping into a noose till an arrow pierces his liver, like a bird darting into a snare, little knowing it will cost him his life. Now then, my sons, listen to me; pay attention to what I say. Do not let your heart turn to her ways or stray into her paths. Many are the victims she has brought down; her slain are a mighty throng. Her house is a highway to the grave, leading down to the chambers of death.

In this passage, we find a narrative showing how a seductress operates. Let me discuss these techniques used by seductresses in some detail.

Language. We see that seductresses use language to entice men. As we read she has "seductive words" and later "with persuasive words she led him astray; she seduced him with her smooth talk." There is, then, a recognition that seduction involves, among other things, persuasion. In the story being told, we are dealing with a youth that lacks judgment so he is, we must assume, assure, relatively easy to persuade.

Dress. The woman is "dressed like a prostitute" which we can take to mean in a manner to enflame the passions and as a signifier of what might be described as her loose morality. We know that clothes can be used as a sexual turn on. Interestingly enough, being naked is not, for most men, as stimulating sexually as wearing clothes that reveal the contours of the body, show a woman's legs, her rear end, her cleavage and some of her breasts.

Assertiveness. We read that the seductress comes out to meet a young man who lacked judgment and "took hold of him." Thus, the seductress is shown to be an assertive woman who is very forward and, in a sense, "attacks" men she wishes to seduce. Taking "hold" of him may also be understood as, in some way, gaining control of him.

Kissing. The seductress kisses her victim, thus getting him sexually excited. The important thing here is that there is physical contact between the seductress and the man she wishes to seduce. Physical contact, the pressure of one's lips upon another and one's body upon another, functions as a means of arousing a person sexually.

Perfume. "I have perfumed my bed with myrrh, aloes and cinnamon," she tells her victim. Thus, she makes use of the power of smell to arouse sexual desire. Smell, we know, is basic to animal sexual behavior; when female animals are in estrus, they signal that by generating certain odors which male animals pick up. In recent years we have learned that smell also plays an important role in human sexuality…not only through artificial means, such as perfumes, but also in terms of subtle and body smells that women give off, of which both men and the women generally are unaware, it turns out.

(Research indicates that women secrete subtle sexually exciting odors from their vaginas that are recognized by men's olfactory receptors. Douching has the effect of ridding the body of these odors and thus, sexually speaking, is an inhibitory action.) We are, after all, animals and there is no reason to think that we do not share, with the lower animals, certain behavioral traits connected with smell and sexuality and other matters as well.

The heart. Proverbs 7 tells the possible victims of a seduction, "Do not let your heart turn to her ways." This suggests that the seductress attempts to sway her victims by emotional appeals, by appeals to feelings and desires, and to avoid letting her victims act rationally. Seductresses have the ability to play upon men's heartstrings and tempt them to do irrational and self-destructive acts, for consorting with them leads, we are told, "to the chambers of death."

Freud has suggested that the psyche is divided into three parts: the id (desire, our drives), the ego (rationality, dealing with reality) and the superego (conscience, guilt). Generally speaking, the ego mediates between the id and the superego and tries to keep them in balance. We need the id because it gives us energy and we need the superego because it prevents us from just wasting our times in pleasurable pursuits. According to Freud, the price we pay for civilization is the suppression of our desire for free sexuality.

The seductress appeals to id elements in our psyches and overwhelms, using the various methods described above, both the superego and the ego. Proverbs 7 (and other proverbs as well) are superego tales, meant to show us…in very graphic form…the dangers involved in going astray. In a broader sense, the cautionary tales about seductresses involve the matter of controlling our sexuality so that we can create civilizations.

As Freud writes in *New Introductory Lectures on Psychoanalysis* (1965:110):

> It has become our habit to say that our civilization has been built up at the cost of sexual trends which, being inhibited to society, are partly, it is true, repressed but have partly been made usable for other aims. We have admitted, too, that, in spite of all our pride in our cultural attainments, it is not easy for us to fulfill the requirements of this civilization or to feel comfortable in it, because the instinctual restrictions imposed on us constitute a heavy psychical burden. Well, what we have come to see about the sexual instincts, applies equally and perhaps still more to the other ones, the aggressive instincts. It is they above all that make human communal life difficult and threaten its survival.

Thus, the seductress can be seen not only as a danger to individuals with whom she consorts but also as a threat to civilization because of two things: her desire for free sexuality and her assertiveness (or aggressiveness), both of which are linked together.

We are able to survive in societies because we gain control of both by the superego and guilt. As Freud has explained this in *Civilization and Its Discontents* as follows:

> Civilization, therefore, obtains mastery of the individual's dangerous desire for aggression by weakening and disarming it

and by setting up an agency within him to watch over it, like a garrison in a conquered city. (1962:70-71)

Seductresses, then, are doubly dangerous, which explains why the Bible is so adamant in cautioning men to avoid them.

Although it does not explicitly deal with the seductress as a threat to society, that is the subtext to be found in this story and in all the stories in the Bible that deal with seductresses. Civilization is built not only upon the suppression of sexuality, but also, we find, upon the suppression of assertive women. That may help explain why Lilith, the monster who seduced men when they are alone in a house and who strangles innocent babies, is seen as one of the heroines of the feminist movement.

Ovid and the Art of Love: The Poetics of Seduction

Ovid was born on March 20, 43 BC in Sulmo, Italy and died in Tomis in 17 AD. He is most famous for his love poems, his *Metamorphoses,* and his treatises on love, the most important...for our purposes...being *The Art of Love.* This work has three parts: the first book is on how men can attract women, the second book is on how men can keep women, and the third book is on how women can attract men. He points out, in the first lines of book one, that love is an art:

Who in this town knows not the lover's art

Should read this book, and play an expert's part.

It's art that speeds the boat with oars and sails,

Art drives the chariot, art in love prevails.

What is important to remember about *The Art of Love* is that it is, first of all, a great work of art, written in a special form of rhymed verse. At the same time, it is a fascinating and highly systematic manual on sexual relations. Ovid's advice, you will see, is as pertinent now as it was 2000 years ago, when he wrote *The Art of Love.*

Virgil had written: Omnia vincit Amor: et nos cedamus Amori. (Love conquers everything: we too must yield to love.) and Ovid had responded: Et mihi cedet Amor. (Love too shall yield to me.) There is good reason to believe that Ovid was right.

The Voice of Experience

Ovid tells us that he writes on the basis of experience, which suggests that we should take his advice seriously. He also offers a prayer that all writers make…to have enough material to write his book:

Experience prompts my labours. Heed the sage:

With truths, oh Venus! help me fill my page.

A.D. Melville, an English scholar, made the translation of the lines from Ovid quoted above. He tried to capture the flavor of Ovid's poetry and his use of the elegiac couplet and rhyme. Some other translations of Ovid don't do this but transpose Ovid's poetry into prose. I will use a prose translation by Walter S. Keating in many places because it makes it easier to understand Ovid's points, though in doing so we lose the means by which he expressed his ideas.

Let me list and paraphrase some of the main points Ovid makes and, from time to time, quote him…generally in the Keating translation but sometimes using Melville's. What we have here, in essence, is a manual for the seductress who wishes to entrance, captivate and capture a man. Ovid reveals himself as a shrewd and calculating individual with incredible insights into the human psyche.

1. Pay attention to your dress. Most women are not beautiful and if you aren't, you must do all you can to dress well.

2. Don't wear too much jewelry or dresses that have too much gold embroidery on them. Men are captivated by neatness.

3. Be careful about how you comb your hair. If you have round features, tie a knot of hair on the top of your head, so your ears will be exposed. In some cases, it is best to let your locks flow loosely.

4. If your hair is gray, dye it or if you need to, use a wig.

5. Wear clothing that doesn't cost too much to dye certain colors. It's best to use natural colors.

6. Shave your legs and your armpits.

7. Brush your teeth every morning, but not in the presence of your lover.

8. Use makeup, but don't let your lover see that you use it or see you putting it on. He adds, "'Tis no harm, too, to mark the eyes slightly with ashes; or with saffron...."

9. It is okay to brush your hair in the presence of your lover, so he can see it flowing behind your back.

10. Conceal your blemishes and bodily imperfections. He writes, "If you are short, sit down; that while standing, you may not appear to be sitting; and if of a diminutive size, throw yourself upon your couch."

11. If you're too thin, wear clothes with a thick texture and let them hang loosely from your shoulders.

12. If you're pale, tint your complexion with purple stripes.

13. Conceal an ill shaped foot in a snow-white leather boot.

14. If you have black teeth or teeth that are too large, only open your mouth a little bit when you laugh...and when you laugh, only utter "sounds gentle and feminine."

15. Learn how to pronounce words correctly.

16. Walk with a gait suited to a woman in a graceful manner.

17. "Let the lower part of your shoulders, and the upper part of your arm be bare," to entice men.

18. The voice has an "insinuating" quality so learn how to speak beautifully and also learn how to sing.

19. Learn to dance.

20. "Devise a thousand amusements." Learn how to play games and how to entertain and amuse men. Men often succumb to women when playing games with them, Ovid tells us.

21. Be sociable and get around a lot; make sure that you're seen in public. "All advantage is lost, when a pretty face is without one to see it," Ovid reminds us.

22. Always be desirous to please and ready to take advantage of what chance brings your way. "Chance is powerful everywhere; let your hook be always hanging ready."

23. Avoid knavish men, who will be unfaithful or who are after your money. Don't believe what they tell you, either.

24. Don't be too quick to answer love letters, but don't wait too long, either. "Delay ever stimulates those in love, if it lasts only a short time." Examine letters carefully to determine whether they are sincere or false.

25. Cause men to both fear and hope at the same time, and if you refuse a man, make sure you give him hope and reason to continue courting you at the same time.

26. Deceit is acceptable to repel deceit on a man's part. In essence Ovid argues that it is okay to fight fire with fire.

27. Avoid getting angry. It will distort your features and make you repulsive.

28. Be cheerful. Remember, the cheerful woman captivates.

29. Remind your lover that he is the only one you love. If he feels he has a rival, "his passion will grow effete."

30. Use wine to get those who are your keepers drunk. Send messages to your lover using a confidante using invisible ink, if necessary.

31. Be careful when you eat. At banquets, come late since delay is a friend to passion. Make sure the person you wish to make love with

has a lot to drink. "Even should you be ugly, to the tipsy you will appear charming."

32. When having sex, consider how to make the most of your positive attributes.

In the last 40 or 50 lines of *The Art of Love,* Ovid discusses how to have sex and how a woman can maximize her impact on her partner while doing so. He stresses that there are many different positions one can adopt during the sex act…"there's no single norm." I will quote from some of this material in the Melville translation:

Know each your person: there's no single norm

For all: let posture to physique conform.

Recline face upwards, you who're fair of face,

Display your back, who back's your chiefest grace.

Well-shapen legs on shoulders should be laid;

Milanion thus with Atalanta's played.

Who's short should ride a-cockhorse: Hector's bride

Was far too tall to sit her horse astride.

Whom the long hip-line graces, on the bed

Should kneel and slightly backward bend her head,

While youthful thighs and faultless breasts demand

That you lie slantwise and your lover stand. (1990:148)

We see, then, that Ovid has thought out everything, and offers a very detailed guide to the woman who wishes too "hook" a man (and that term can mean "seduce") that is full of shrewd calculations and wise counsel. It is very much like the articles we see in many women's magazines about beauty tricks and how to keep a man happy and make him sexually fulfilled.

Seduction, we are told by Ovid, is an art. And the seductress is an artist who uses her beauty, fashion, cosmetics, her mind, her personality, the particular nature of her body, and many other things that Ovid tells us about…to achieve her aims. Armed with Ovid's shrewd tactics, seducing a man seems almost as easy as shooting fish in a barrel, and he makes the analogy between men and fish…both need to be hooked and one should always be ready to do so.

Is Seduction Essentially the Same Everywhere or Are There Many Different Kinds of Seductions

My mention of seduction and nationality, social class, religion, climate, and my discussion of the techniques of seduction raises an important question about seduction. Is there an archetype of feminine seduction, a basic, universal method used by all women (with only minor differences here and there), or are there significant variations so that French seduction techniques vary considerably from, say, American seduction techniques or Japanese seduction techniques. The answer to this question is to see how women have seduced men throughout history and how seduction is portrayed in works of literature and the arts, in myth, in folklore…from different countries.

We also must make a distinction between seduction, prostitution and courtesanship. Seduction, in the most primal sense of the term, as we will understand it, ultimately is based on arousal and passion. But that passion may be the result of a lot of planning and calculating by the seductress. Prostitution is sex for payment by any customer. Courtesans are different from prostitutes in that they choose their lovers and may use seduction to establish some kind of a relationship. The same, generally speaking, applies to mistresses, who may have been seduced by a male or who may have seduced a male.

Most sexual relationships between men and women, of course, are not based on seduction. They are based on physical attraction, interests, compatibility, affection, humor, love…whatever. And when men and women who are dating have sex, it is generally not a matter of seduction but of a mutual desire for sexual pleasure. In some cases, I will admit, it is difficult to make clear-cut distinctions between seductresses, mistresses, courtesans and prostitutes, since each of these relationships may have elements of one-another in them.

Frustrating Seductions as Comedy

As I write this my mind returns to a play I saw many years ago, by Peter Ustinov, called *The Love of Four Colonels*. In this play, four colonels, each from different countries (France, England, Russia and America), use techniques congruent with their national cultures, to attempt to seduce a beautiful woman. It was a comedy and therefore all the seduction attempts were frustrated.

It is rather interesting to think that in America (and perhaps in many other countries) a great deal of comedy involves frustrating attempts at seduction. One of the basic techniques of humor involves disappointments and defeated expectations (especially, it seems, frustrations of a sexual nature).

That is one of the main themes of the American situation comedy *Frasier*, which has won many awards for the quality of its writing and performances by its actors and actresses. The lead character, Frasier, a psychiatrist, is always attempting to seduce women. (His ex-wife, and this is of considerable symbolic significance, is named Lilith.) He lures them to his apartment but, for one reason or another, these seduction attempts always fail.

One of the female characters in *Frasier*, Roz, is a man-hungry woman whose sexual needs are very great and who spends a great deal of time chasing men and, so it is suggested, catching a good number of them. She is, it turns out, an extremely beautiful woman so there's something curious about her being characterized as unable to find sexual partners or have a sustained relationship with a man.

Perhaps it is because she is so compulsive? Perhaps it is because men fear a woman who is very open about her sexual needs and desires? In the show Roz always talks about finding the "right" guy, but for one reason or another never is able to do so.

Sociological research also indicates that in America, people see situations in which sexual relations between men and women and seductions are foiled as humorous. (This may be because there is a play frame evident that tells us "this is not real" and we know we are seeing a comedy.) Why this is the case is quite curious. In part it is because, as I pointed out above, frustrating people from doing anything is a basic technique of humor. I would describe this technique as "disappointments and defeated expectations."

There may also be an element of anxiety that we project upon the performers...a fear that having sex or being seduced can lead to all kinds of problems. Whether seduction itself can be comic...in some or all respects...and humorous is, of course, another matter. Can there be comic seductions, or is seduction, by definition, always a very serious matter?

The fact that Aphrodite, the goddess of love and beauty, is also known as the laughing goddess, should give us a hint. If we now see sex as, in certain respects, involving play and as a kind of game, it is quite possible to see seduction as being, in certain cases, humorous. It is possible, for example, that seductresses use wit and humor as a means of disguising their intentions, making light of the matter of sexual relations, and evading the inhibitions or anxieties that some males may have about sex.

In most cases, however, seduction is portrayed as very serious in nature and seductresses are seen as dangerous women who have a magical power to entrance and ultimately destroy men.

Part I:

Seductresses in the Bible and Folklore

CHAPTER 2

JUDITH: A SEDUCTRESS WHO GOT AHEAD IN THE WORLD

Judith is a story told in the Apocrypha, a part of the Bible that is not considered important for doctrinal matters but, rather, for edification. And like Delilah and Salome, the consequences of being tempted turn out to be quite negative, as far as men are concerned. Readers of the Bible are given good cause to fear being tempted, for the consequences of sin tend, almost always, to be rather horrific.

Judith's Story

The story of Judith starts off with king Nabuchodonosor of the Assyrians, who decides to "avenge himself on all the earth." He tells Holofernes, the head of his army, to assemble an army and punish those lands where people did not obey his commandments. Holofernes creates an army and goes off destroying one place after another. He destroyed:

> Phud and Lud, and spoiled all the children of Rasses, and the children of Ismael, which were toward the wilderness at the south of the land of the Chellians. Then he went over Euphrates, and went through Mesopotamia, and destroyed all the high cities that were upon the river Arbonai, till ye come to the sea.

He continues on like this through the plain of Damascus until he comes to Israel, where the people have decided to resist him. They have heard what he has done in other lands and were worried about what he would do to them. So the people of Israel fortify themselves on mountain tops, where it would be difficult to beat them. They have brought food and cisterns of water, also.

Holofernes is given advice by some advisors. They tell him not to fight the Israelites on the mountain tops but prevent them from getting water and thus force them to surrender when they are dying of thirst. They tell him:

> Remain in thy camp, and keep all the men of thine army, and let thy servants get into their hands the fountain of water which issueth forth of the foot of the mountain.

Holofernes's "servants" go and camp all around the Israelites and cut off their water supplies. Eventually, the Israelites run out of water and decide to surrender to Holofernes rather than dying because they had no water. Ozias, the leader of the Jews, agrees to do so if they haven't had rain to fill their cisterns in the nest five days.

It is here that Judith enters the story. She is a widower whose husband has died three years earlier. She had made a tent on the top of her house, had put on widow's apparel and fasted. Judith is described as being of "a goodly countenance, and very beautiful to behold." She hears about the situation and decides to take action. She tells Ozias that she will save her people:

> Hear me, and I will do a thing, which shall go throughout all generations to the children of our nation. Ye shall stand this night in the gate, and I will go forth with my waitingwoman: and with the days that ye have promised to deliver the city to our enemies the Lord will visit Israel by my hand. But enquire not ye of mine act: for I will not declare it unto you, till the things be finished that I do.

She then prays to God that she can be the instrument of her people's salvation and prevent the Assyrians from desecrating the Tabernacle.

Smite by the deceit of my lips the servant with the prince, and the prince with the servant: break down their stateliness by the hand of a woman.

Then Judith prepares for battle. These are some of the things she does to enable her to accomplish her mission:

1. She takes off her clothes of widowhood.

2. She washes her body all over with water.

3. She anoints herself with precious ointments

4. She braids her hair

5. She puts on her garments of gladness

6. She puts on her bracelets, her chains, her rings, her earrings and all her ornaments "to allure the eyes of all men that should see her."

Judith is a beautiful woman who knows she can use her beauty to achieve her goal. When she goes out of her house with her maid, those who saw her "wondered at her beauty very greatly."

She leaves the city and shortly arrives at the camp of the Assyrians.

She tells them that she is a "woman of the Hebrews" who has fled from them and that she can show Holofernes a way to defeat the Jews who are encamped in the Hill country without losing any men.

The guards are overcome by her beauty and bring her to Holofernes, where they tell him about Judith. We find the following description of Judith and the thoughts her beauty created in the minds of the Assyrians:

And they wondered at her beauty, and admired the children of Israel because of her, and every one said to his neighbour, "Who would despise this people, that have among them such women? surely it is not good that one man of them be left, who, being let go, might deceive the whole earth."

She is ushered in to Holofernes' tent, where he is lying upon his bed under a canopy woven with gold, emeralds and precious stones. When they see her "they all marveled at the beauty of her countenance."

She then speaks to him:

Receive the words of they servant, and suffer thy handmaid to speak in thy presence, and I will declare no lie to my lord this night. And if thou wilt follow the words of thine handmaid, God will bring the things perfectly to pass by thee; and my lord shall not fail of his purposes.

She continues on in this manner, in words that it turns out are highly ambiguous. Her words are very pleasing to Holofernes and his servants who proclaim, "There is not such a woman from end of the earth to the other, both for beauty of ace, and wisdom of words."

Holofernes becomes smitten by her, and we read, "his heart was ravished with her, and his mind was moved, and he desired greatly her company: for he waited a time to deceive her, from the day that he had seen her." Holofernes is consumed by lust and desire for Judith. He tells her to drink and be merry with him and his men and she does so. He becomes very drunk, having consumed more wine than he'd ever drunk before.

Later, the party ends and everyone leaves Holofernes's tent except Judith, who is described as "lying along upon is bed: for he was filled with wine." Judith, who had told her maid to wait outside the tent, then goes into action:

Then she came to the pillar of the bed, which was at Holofernes's head, and took down his falchion from thence, and approached to his bed, and took hold of the hair of his head, and said, "Strengthen me, O Lord God of Israel, this day." and she smote twice upon his neck with all her might, and she took away his head from him, and tumbled his body down from the bed, and pulled down the canopy from the pillars; and anon after she went forth, and gave Holofernes his head to her maid. And she put it in her bag of meat.

Judith then brings Holofernes's head to the Hebrews, telling them that the Lord "hath smitten him by the hand of a woman."

The Lessons of Judith's Seduction

From this story we draw a number of morals. First, we see that in some cases seduction can be used for good purposes. It also can be used for evil ones, as well. In our fictions dealing with spying and espionage, many beautiful women turn out to be spies who use their beauty and sexuality to help compromise politicians, generals, and others who have information (secrets, codes, plans for military operations, etc.) of use to the organization that is using the spy.

Second, we learn about what it is that enabled Judith to "seduce" Holofernes. She was extremely beautiful, she dressed in a manner to emphasize her beauty, with jewelry and other adornments. And she was, as Holofernes put it, "witty" in her words. Her beauty turned Holofernes' head (in more ways than one, it turns out) and weakened his judgment...he drank too much wine and thus was unable to prevent Judith from decapitating him.

Wine and women, we learn, are not always a good combination.

A Short Footnote on Seduction and Ethics

Ethics is a very complicated subject. There are considerable disagreements among professional ethicists and among the general public, about what is and what is not ethical behavior. For example, some ethicists argue that behavior is relative to cultures. Thus "when in France, do as the French do." Other ethicists are absolutists and argue that certain behavior is wrong, even if it is considered acceptable in certain cultures or among certain groups. If there are standards of right behavior that should be applied to all people, that are absolute, how do we determine them?

We also make a distinction between laws and morals. One obeys laws for a variety of reasons, such as the fact that we can be punished for disobeying them. Moral behavior is a different matter. for it involves our evaluating possible actions and deciding which actions are good and which ones are evil. Just because something is legal doesn't mean it is moral; for example, once slavery was legal. But it was still immoral and thus someone who fought against slavery was acting morally, though perhaps illegally.

The Problem of Means and Ends

One commonly understood principle of ethics is that people should be used as "ends" not "means to an end." That is, we shouldn't *use* people for our own purposes. Thus, we should be friends with people because we like them, not because they can be helpful in getting a job or because they can be of use to us in some other manner. We should associate with people because we like who they are not what they can do for us.

This would suggest that women who seduce men (and vice versa) which involves "using" someone else for sexual gratification and possibly for other means, are acting in an unethical manner. They are not treating the men they seduce as "ends," but are using them for their own purposes: sexual gratification and perhaps something else as well.

In addition, there is the problem that arises when a woman seduces a male who is married or even engaged to someone else. A married man who is seduced by a woman becomes an adulterer…a man who is unfaithful to his wife (and his family) or his fiancée, if he is engaged. Thus, he violates the trust that has been placed in him and this, most ethicists would argue, is an example of immoral behavior.

But what about women like Judith, who seduces a man to save her people? Is this an ethical act?

The Problem of Judith

Judith seduces an Assyrian general, Holofernes, so she can save her people from destruction. He is overwhelmed by her beauty and loses any sense of restraint. He drinks too much so he becomes powerless. And then Judith cuts off his head. So we have in Judith a seductress and a murderess who has become a great heroine. How can we explain this?

The answer is that in beheading Holofernes Judith was saving the Jews from a tyrant who would have killed many people and destroyed the Temple. Thus, unless you consider killing to be wrong under any circumstances…that is, the commandment "Thou shall not kill" is an absolute

that must be followed in all cases. If this commandment is an absolute, we cannot protect ourselves against a person who attempts to kill us. What we do is use the notion that we shouldn't kill as a general rule of conduct, but recognize that it is right to kill in self-defense.

If killing Holofernes is considered to be a moral act, and can be construed as an act of self-defense, then using seduction as a means to obtain this end becomes a moral act as well. So seduction can, in certain circumstances, be recognized as a moral act. We can make the same point about women spies who seduced Japanese or German soldiers and military officers during the Second World War to obtain valuable information to aid us in our fight against the Axis powers.

There is, in much of our popular culture…especially in a number of films…a strong connection between seduction and killing, as vamps destroy the men they have seduced and their sisters in seduction, vampires, actually kill their victims. But this kind of killing is not moral.

One can, perhaps, argue that showing how dangerous seductresses are, so as to persuade men to avoid becoming involved with them, is a moral act on the part of the novelist or film-maker. In many films, the consequence of seduction is death.

Technology and Seductresses

It is quite likely that women have become bolder in their sexual relationships due to new technological developments such as the birth control pill and intrauterine devices. They free women from the fear of becoming pregnant after having sex.

Thus, it is possible that now that women have gained the power to control contraception…a power that used to be controlled by men, through the use of condoms…they have felt more enabled to take the initiative and become seductresses. This would just be one more example of the power of technology to affect moral behavior.

In his book *Desexualization in American Life,* anthropologist Charles Winick has an amusing description of a fashion that was popular a number of years ago, the so-called "wet" look. As Winick writes (199 :317)

We may speculate that one reason for the current success of women's

dresses, coats, and boots of vinyl, in spite of the material's stiffness and non-porousness, could be that a woman in vinyl somewhat resembles a penis sheathed in a condom.

Thus, our seductress, dressed in her vinyl dress, coat and boots, now resembles a penis in a condom. She thus functions as a "turn on" for men she wishes to seduce…reminding them that they could be putting on a condom to use with her.

It is possible to argue, then, that the behavior of seductresses is often morally ambiguous. Thus, a woman who seduces a man can, in certain circumstances, do so for moral reasons: to save her people, to prevent evil acts, or even to help the male who has been seduced. And also, there is the fact that the seductress while giving pleasure to herself also, at the same time, gives pleasure to the male who has been seduced.

So we have to be careful when we consider the moral aspects of seduction. They often are much more complicated than we might imagine and we do violence to things when we assume, automatically, that seductresses are always acting in an immoral nature.

CHAPTER 3

SCHEHEREZADE: THE SEDUCTRESS AS SEX THERAPIST

The story of Scheherezade, also known as the "One Thousand and One Nights," comes from India and Persia and was told as early as the tenth century. As we will see, like many fairy tales, there's more to the story than we might imagine.

Scheherezade: The Fairy Tale

A king, Shahryar has become disillusioned with women when he discovers that he wife has betrayed him with slaves and that the same thing has happened to his brother, Shahzeman. In addition, he finds out that a powerful and sly Jinny has also been betrayed by a woman who he had believed was locked up and away from temptation.

Shahryar decided that he won't give women the opportunity to betray him again and that he will abandon love and live only to satisfy his lustful desires. His plan is simple: he will sleep each night with a virgin who will be killed the next morning. When he has slept with and killed all of the virgins in his land, except one, it becomes Scheherezade's turn. She is the daughter of the king's vizier.

The vizier pleads with her to leave the country but she tells her father that she will find a way to deliver the women in the kingdom from the king and to save the king from his hateful and destructive behavior. She does this as follows: each night she starts telling the king a story, but arranges to be interrupted, after the king and her have sex, by her little sister Dunayazad, who asks Scheherezade to tell her a story. She always starts a story but never has time to finish it. Thus, she has to finish the story the next evening. That evening she finishes her story and starts another one. The king is so delighted by her stories that he wants to hear how they end. And no sooner does Scheherezade end one story than she starts another.

After a thousand and one nights of telling the king stories, he has given up his hatred of women and fallen in love with Scheherezade. She has also given birth to a little boy. They all live happily ever after, in the best traditions of fairy tales.

A Psychoanalytic Interpretation of a Thousand and One Nights

Bruno Bettelheim has analyzed this story in his book *The Uses of Enchantment: The Meaning and Importance of Fairy Tales*. He describes the two main characters in this story, Scheherezade and the king, as follows: (1976:88)

> The king symbolizes a person completely dominated by his id because his ego, due to severe disappointments in life, has lost its strength to keep his id in bounds....Scheherezade represents the ego, as is clearly suggested by our being told that "she had collected a thousand books of chronicles of past peoples and bygone poets. Moreover, she had read books of science and medicine; her memory was stored with verses and stories and folklore and the sayings of kings and sages, and she was wise, witty, prudent and well-bred"...an exhaustive enumeration of ego attributes.

Bettelheim suggests, here, that the king's id has lost the ability to draw on the positive energy of his ego for positive purposes and has given in to the murderous propensities of his id. The stories that Scheherezade tells the king help him become more integrated and give him enough ego strength so he can learn to dominate the negative aspects of his id.

This interpretation is based on the notion that the psyche has three forces in it: the id (desire, lust), the ego (rationality), and the superego (conscience, guilt). There is always a battle going on between the id elements of our psyches and the superego elements of our psyches. The ego mediates between these two forces and tries to arrange a balance, so that we aren't overwhelmed by either desire or guilt. We need the id to give us energy, but we cannot allow it free reign, and we need the superego to give us morality, but if it becomes too powerful we become incapable of doing anything. What the ego must do if find a way to help us balance these contending forces of id and superego, by developing enough ego strength so we can become integrated personalities.

Slow-Motion Seduction

It is reasonable to suggest that Scheherezade seduced the king…in the best possible understanding of the term. The king had sex with her from the first day, but it was based on lust and carnal desire. He was so bitter about women that he had all the virgins he slept with killed the next day…insuring that he would not be betrayed.

In this story, we find a different kind of seduction than we find in most of the stories dealt with in this book. The sex comes *before* the seduction and the seduction is positive in nature. One might even propose that Scheherezade was one of the first sex therapists; she used sexual intercourse along with story telling to save the king from his anger, disgust with life, and his fear that nobody could love him.

The stories Scheherezade told not only entertained him but also taught him about life and love, so that eventually he was able to overcome his grief and find a way to integrate his personality. And Scheherezade, who faced a crisis herself…namely immanent death…was able to find someone to love, also.

It is not often that we can say that seduction is an ego function; usually we see seduction as an id-dominated activity that after a short period of sexual excitement leads to sexual relations. Here things are backwards: we have sexual relations as a given and story-telling (that is, a particular form of talk or conversation in the broadest sense of the term) as something that seems like…but isn't, we know…a kind of afterthought.

The Time-Factor

Scheherezade took a thousand and one nights to seduce King Shahryar; it ranks as probably the slowest, least hurried, most deliberately carried out seduction by anyone…male or female…on record. It took almost two and a half years! This seduction was not, in essence, sexual in nature though the relationship of Scheherezade and Shaharyar was, at least at the beginning, a sexual one.

Some seductions are strategically planned, such as Madame de Pompadour's campaign to attract the attention of King Louis XV of France and, at a propitious moment, to lead him to her bed. But she did not spend more than two years arranging to get at the king.

It is conceivable that many real-life seductions also have an extremely long-range time frame. The actual process of a woman inducing a man to go to bed with her may not take very long…perhaps less than an evening. But it might take a considerable amount of time to maneuver the man into a situation where he is physically present in the right place and the situation is optimal and he actually can be seduced.

What We Learn From Scheherezade

There are several important things we learn from Scheherezade. First, we see that language, the ability to converse, the skill a woman has in telling stories, plays a very important part in the seduction process. Great seductresses are often women who can entrance a man with their conversational skills and use of language. They may be witty and often are quite entertaining. We must always keep in mind that Aphrodite was always describe as laughing. So conversational ability is important.

Second, we find that sometimes seductions are based on strategic thinking. In some cases women plan long term campaigns to get the right conditions, ones that involve physical proximity (unless one is satisfied with virtual seduction, but like virtual food, virtual seduction isn't very satisfying) and privacy. It might seem strange to talk about seduction in terms of strategic thinking, but it was her ability to think strategically which saved Scheherezade.

The actual seduction, as I suggested earlier, may not take very much time, but making the arrangements and luring the man to be seduced to the right place, where he can be seduced, may be quite complicated and take a great deal of planning. There is something almost clinical about this kind of thing; one thinks of a spider weaving a web for some unsuspecting bug to get stuck on or a female black widow spider luring a frightened and pathetic pip-squeak of a male black widow spider into the mating process. He cannot resist having sex with her, but at great peril. She will, as we know, eat the male after he has had sex with her unless he can escape from her. Huge female insects devouring tiny male ones is not unusual in the insect kingdom. The third thing we learn from Scheherezade is that seductions can, in certain circumstances, be humane and positive in nature. The term seduction has negative connotations, which are justified in most cases...but not always. Therapy can be looked upon as a kind of seduction and in the story of a Thousand and One Nights, Scheherezade's seduction of the king can be looked upon as therapy.

Part II:

Seductresses in History

CHAPTER 4

CLEOPATRA: THE SEDUCTRESS AS TRAGIC FIGURE

Cleopatra is probably one of the most famous seductress of all time, whose life was dramatized by Shakespeare's *Anthony and Cleopatra* and made into a heroine of mass culture in the 1963 film, *Cleopatra,* with Elizabeth Taylor playing the role of Cleopatra. She remains an enigmatic figure, whose name is familiar to many but about whom most people know relatively little.

A Portrait of Cleopatra

Cleopatra was the daughter of King Ptolmey XI. He gave his throne to his children Ptolmey XII and Cleopatra, whom he wanted to marry and rule together. Cleopatra was, it is thought, most likely a blonde and an enchanting but not strikingly beautiful woman. (Some historians, I should point out, have speculated that she was black, coming from Egypt.) The historian Will Durant describes her in *Caesar and Christ* as follows: (Simon & Schuster, 1944:184)

> She was not particularly beautiful; but the grace of her carriage, the vivacity of her body and her mind, the variety of her accomplishments, the suavity of her manners, the very melody of her voice, combined with her royal position to make her a heady wine even for a Roman general. She was acquainted with Greek history, literature, and philosophy; she spoke Greek, Egyptian, Syrian, and allegedly other languages, well; she added the intellectual fascination of an Aspasia to the seductive abandon of a

41

completely uninhibited woman. Tradition credits her with a treatise of cosmetics and another on the alluring subject of Egyptian measures, weights, and coins. She was an able ruler and administrator, effectively promoted Egyptian commerce and industry, and was a competent financier even when making love. With these qualities went an Oriental sensuality, an impetuous brutality that dealt out suffering and death, and a political ambition that dreamed of empire and honored no code but success.

She was also resourceful, for the story goes that when she was banished, Caesar secretly sent for her. She arranged to be smuggled to Caesar by hiding in some bedding which her attendant, Appollodorus, brought to Caesar.

Durant gives us what he imagined to be Caesar's response: The amazed Roman, who never let his victories in the field outnumber his conquests in love, was captivated by her courage and wit.

Caesar fell under her spell and it is reported that he often feasted with her all night long. In 47 BC she bore him a child, Caesarion, whom Caesar acknowledged was his son.

A few years later, in 42 BC, after the battle of Phillipi, Mark Antony was made ruler of Egypt. He ordered Cleopatra to come before him at Tarsus, to answer certain charges that had been made against her. Here is Durant's description of how Cleopatra arrived at Tarsus: (1944:204)

While Antony sat on a throne in the forum waiting for her to plead and be judged, she sailed up the river Cydnus in a barge with purple sails, gilded stern, and silver oars that beat time to the music of flutes and fifes and harps. Her maids, dressed as sea nymphs and graces, were the crew, while she herself, dressed as Venus, lay under a canopy of cloth of gold. When the news of this seductive apparition spread among the people of Tarsus, they flocked to the shore, leaving Antony solitary on his throne. Cleopatra invited him to dine with her on her ship. He came with an overawing retinue; she feted them with every luxury, and corrupted his general with gifts and smiles. Antony had almost fallen in love with her as a girl in Alexandria; now he found her, at twenty-nine, in the full maturity of her charms. He began with reproving her, and ended by presenting her with Phoenecia, Coele-Syria, Cyprus, and parts of Arabia, Cilicia, and Judea. She rewarded him according to his desire and invited him to Alexandria. There he spent a carefree winter, drinking the Queen's love, listening to lectures at the Museum, and forgetting that he had an empire to rule.

We have here, in these descriptions of Cleopatra and her behavior, a superb example of the seductress in action. Antony was by no means innocent; he was known to be a rather wild sensualist who spent his time partying and carousing with loose women. (Her relationship with Antony proved to be disastrous. He stabbed himself when he was told she was dead, only to find out that she was still alive. He was brought to her and, so the story goes, died in her arms. Then Cleopatra committed suicide by pressing a poisonous asp to her breast. In this case, the seductress as well as the seduced male died.)

Cleopatra's Techniques of Seduction

The passages quoted above were based on Roman sources that Durant used to get his information about Cleopatra, Caesar, and Antony. On the basis of these sources, we can describe Cleopatra as a consummate enchantress, who brilliantly mastered and employed the techniques of the seductress. Let us consider Cleopatra as a seductress.

She was an attractive woman. The author says she was "not particularly beautiful" which suggests she could be described as somewhere between beautiful and attractive. It's always an advantage to be beautiful if you're a seductress, and many of the great seductresses are beautiful. We can't be sure how beautiful she was, but she was known to dress flamboyantly and use a great deal of makeup to glamorize herself. She is known to have had her feet massaged with scented oils by her slaves and dried with peacock feathers. From head to foot she was a sensual being.

She carried herself well. Durant mentions "the grace of her carriage," which is important, because the way a woman walks and her sense of herself play an important role in the way a male perceives her. Her "vivacious" body, or what we would now call her use of body language, thus, is an important attribute.

She had suave manners. Cleopatra was, obviously, a woman of accomplishment and sophistication, which showed up in her manners. Unlike some seductresses who represent little but animal sensuality, Cleopatra was a person whose refinement added to her attractiveness and her allure.

She had a "melodious" voice. Time and time again we find that seductresses convey their sensuality and sexual desire and attract men not only by what they say but also by the quality of their voice. The Sirens are the most important example of the power of voice to seduce men. And seductresses know how powerful the human voice is in generating emotions in people.

She knew Greek history, literature and philosophy and spoke a number of languages. In addition to her physical attributes, Cleopatra was an educated woman who, one must assume, could charm men with her knowledge and converse with them about philosophy and other heady matters. She was also reputed to be witty.

She was a completely uninhibited woman. What is particularly fascinating about Cleopatra is that in addition to all her intelligence, sophistication and charm, she was also sexually uninhibited. As such she may serve as the prototype of the educated and sophisticated seductress, as contrasted to the "savage" seductress, who lacks education and represents a kind of sheer animality, and the "demon" seductress, who uses her powers to destroy men.

She had a theatrical sensibility. We see this in the remarkable scene in which she sails her barge up the Cydnus river with her maids dressed as sea nymphs and displays herself, as Venus, the goddess of love, lying under a canopy of gold. This theatrical sensibility is often found in seductresses, who bedeck themselves with jewelry and other ornaments and dress in a manner to attract attention and desire.

She offers food and drink to those she wishes to seduce. Cleopatra invites Antony and his generals to dine with her on her barge, where she feeds them royally and gives them many gifts. Often there is wine involved in seductions…since good food and wine (and other forms of alcohol) lower the resistance men have to seductresses.

She has sex with Antony. Durant says "she rewarded him according to his desires" which means she and Antony had sex. This seduction was not a one-time event, since there was political advantage to be gained by having a liaison with Antony. She is reported to have had twins from her relations with Antony.

There is a wonderful story, probably apocryphal, about Cleopatra and Antony that is recounted in William A. Rossi's *The Sex Life of the Foot and Shoe.* Rossi writes: (1976:12)

> One evening a jealous Mark Antony stormed into Cleopatra's boudoir. She languished on a luxurious couch, clad only in a diaphanous robe. Antony, arms folded firmly across his chest, looked down at her and said sternly "I am here to talk about Caesar." Cleopatra slowly stretched her bare, perfumed foot toward him, toes moving sinuously as though in rhythm with the undulations of the small live snake that was frequently entwined around her ankle. She reached out and touched Antony's naked thigh with the tip of her polished toes. He grasped her foot and covered it with ardent kisses. She looked up and said softly, "Now, I am not prone to argue."

This little story is a testimonial to Cleopatra's sexual appeal, but she didn't do everything for sexual satisfaction.

There was, it would seem, also a political motivation to Cleopatra's behavior, which might temper our judgment of her behavior. As Durant explains: (1944:204)

> She knew that Egypt, rich but weak, would soon attract the cupidity of omnipotent Rome; the only salvation for her country and her throne lay in marriage with Rome's lord. She had sought this with Caesar; she sought it now with Antony.

This offers an important insight that might explain...partially, at least...Cleopatra's behavior. She was, so commentators in her time suggest, a sensualist and an uninhibited woman; she was a rather notorious seductress. But there may also have been, Durant suggests, an element of politics...perhaps even patriotism...behind her behavior.

Cleopatra is, then, an enigmatic figure. It is hard to untangle her sensuality and uninhibited sexuality from her strategic thinking about politics and power and maybe even her patriotism. Whatever the case, she has gone down in history as one of the greatest, most interesting and most flamboyant seductresses of all time.

CHAPTER 5

MESSALINA: A SEDUCTRESS FOR THE AGES

Valeria Messalina, well trained in the arts of decadence and debauchery by her apprenticeship in Caligula's court, married Claudius when she was 16 and he was 50. Physically, Claudius was a mess...he stuttered, limped, drooled and his mind wandered. He also drank a great deal. She was no beauty, either. As Will Durant described her in *Caesar and Christ* (1944:271), she wasn't particularly pretty, with a head that was flat, florid face, and malformed chest. But as Durant explains, you don't have to be beautiful to commit adultery.

Messalina is reported to have fallen in love with a dancer Mnester. He, however, rejected her advances so she begged Claudius to tell Mnester to be obedient to her requests. Claudius agreed, and then Mnester yielded to her as a patriotic act. Messalina recognized the usefulness of this formula, and adopted it with many other men.

One reason Messalina could get away with this kind of behavior was that Claudius was "immoderate in his passion for women" according to the historian Suetonius. And Messalina was clever enough to provide Claudius with some beautiful housemaids to serve as bedfellows. Messalina and Claudius had, it seems, what we would now call an "open" marriage.

Durant recounts a story, no doubt apocryphal, from Juvenal, another great Roman historian, to the effect that Messalina would disguise herself, go to a brothel and receive all comers and pocket their fees. This would suggest that there are elements of nymphomania in Messalina's sexual behavior...but in the Roman courts, where there was so much excess in every sense, it is hard to draw the line between lust and nymphomania.

(This story about her was spread by Messalina's successor, Agrippina, who was also a calculating, devious and seductive woman.)

William A. Rossi, the raconteur of foot fetishists and pedophiliacs, tells a story about Messalina that has a comic touch to it. She wanted to have sex with Lucius, who was the father of the Emperor Vitellus. In their first meeting, Lucius asked her to remove one of her jeweled sandals. Rossi writes in his book *The Sex Life of the Foot and Shoe*: (1976:192)

> He removed one sandal, passionately kissed it, then suddenly ran out of the house with it. He continued to carry the sandal concealed between his robe and tunic, kissing it in private from time to time with rapturous fervor. He was once caught doing this in public, and suddenly he was "exposed." But none recognized him for the shoe fetishist he was. Instead, his sandal-kissing was misinterpreted as a kind of fawning boot licking. And so arose the still-popular expression, "He has kissed Messalina's slipper," referring to anyone who flatters and acts in servilely manner to win favor.

In this story, Messalina's desire for sexual satisfaction was frustrated by Lucius's shoe fetishism, which seems to have been more powerful than his desire for sexual intercourse. Rossi's book deals with shoe and foot fetishism throughout history and he has many stories to tell about the curious ways in which people have related (sexually, that is) to feet and to shoes.

The historian Tacitus provides us with some detailed information about Messalina in his book *The Annals (Chapter XI)*. He writes:

> She had grown so frantically enamoured of Caius Silius, the handsomest of the young nobility of Rome, that she drove from his bed Junia Silana, a high-born lady, and had her lover wholly to herself. Silius was not unconscious of his wickedness and his peril; but a refusal would have insured destruction, and he had some hope of escaping exposure; the prize too was great, so he consoled himself by awaiting the future and enjoying the present. As for

her, careless of concealment, she went continually with a numerous retinue to his house, she haunted his steps, showered on him wealth and honours, and, at last, as though empire had passed to another, the slaves, the freedmen, the very furniture of the emperor were to be seen in the possession of the paramour.

For some reason Silius came to the conclusion that he should make his relationship with Messalina more public. He decided to marry Messalina and adopt her son Brittanicus. Silius didn't want to wait for Claudius to become an old man and die and concluded that an act of audacity…marrying Messalina…was his best course of action. Doing so would also make it possible for Silius to become Emperor.

At first Messalina didn't like this idea because she was afraid that if Silius became emperor, he would spurn her. But she also wanted to be his wife, and so when Claudius went to Ostia to take part in sacrificial rituals there, she married Silius. There is some question about whether Messalina was still married to Claudius. Some historians suggest that she had convinced Claudius to divorce her for a short period of time.

The marriage threw Claudius' court into a panic and its members resolved that Claudius should do something about this threat to their power and to his throne. They induced two of Claudius' mistresses to break the news to him. Tacitus recounts, in some detail, how this was done:

> On this, Calpurnia (that was the woman's name), as soon as she was allowed a private interview, threw herself at the emperor's knees, crying out that Messalina was married to Silius. At the same time she asked Cleopatra, who was standing near and waiting for the question, whether she knew it. Cleopatra nodding assent, she begged that Narcissus might be summoned. Narcissus entreated pardon for the past, for having concealed the scandal…

Claudius, however, was wavering, saying he wouldn't charge Messalina with adultery if Silius would agree to give Messalina back and to have their marriage annulled. Narcissus told Claudius that he had to act immediately or he was in danger of losing his throne. "Do you know," Narcissus said "of your divorce? The people, the army, the Senate saw the marriage of Silius. Act at once, or the new husband is master of Rome."

While Claudius' court was planning to get rid of Messalina, she was celebrating her marriage with wild and orgiastic parties. Then the news came that Claudius and his army was coming, "bent on vengeance." Messalina retreated to the gardens of Lucullus, where she wrote letters of entreaty to Claudius. He, it turns out, was wavering and fearing that he would spare Messalina, Narcissus took things into his own hands and ordered some centurions and tribunes to kill Messalina.

Tacitus describes her death as follows:

> Then for the first time she understood her fate and put her hand to a dagger. In her terror she was applying it ineffectually to her throat and breast, when a blow from the tribune drove it through her. Her body was given up to her mother. Claudius was still at the banquet when they told him that Messalina was dead, without mentioning whether it was by her own or another's hand. Nor did he ask the question, but called for the cup and finished his repast as usual. During the days which followed he showed no sign of hatred or joy or anger or sadness, in a word, of any human emotion, either when he looked on her triumphant accusers or on her weeping children. The Senate assisted his forgetfulness by decreeing that her name and her statues should be removed from all places, public or private.

Thus, Messalina's name was "erased" from Roman history of her day and it was almost as if she had never lived. Claudius is reputed to have never mentioned her name after her death. Messalina had the loyalty of a small group of people who gained power and wealth by allying with her, but the population of Rome hated her and saw her as a corrupt and dissipated adulteress. Some historians have suggested that Messalina chose Silius not because she was enamoured of him but because she was afraid that Claudius would be murdered and so she chose to ally herself with Silius, who was from an aristocratic Roman family.

According to this theory, she believed that an alliance with his family might help her win over the Roman legions and Praetorian Guard. After her death, Claudius is rumored to have told the Praetorian Guard that if he ever got married again, they should feel free to kill him. It wasn't long, however, before Claudius' niece, Agrippina, who was very proficient in the arts of the seductress, enticed him into marriage again, and five years later, poisoned him. Messalina has become an archetype of the dissipated, sexually uninhibited seductress. Messalina's infamy also lives on in medical terminology. Nymphomania, it turns out, is sometimes described by psychiatrists as "the Messalina complex."

CHAPTER 6

THEODORA: THE SEDUCTRESS WHO RULED AND EMPIRE

Theodora was a Byzantine stripper who rose from the gutter to become empress of Byzantium. It is a remarkable story and Theodora was an incredible woman. What we know of her comes from such historians as Procopius, who was her contemporary, and others such as John of Malalas and John of Ephesus.

Theodora's Early Years
We know that Theodora, who was born around 500 A.D., had an older sister, Comito and a younger one, Anastasia. Shortly after Anastasia's birth, Theodora's father, who worked as a bear keeper, died and her mother found another man to take her dead father's place…a man who hoped to inherit Theodora's father's job as a bear keeper. When Theodora's mother went to inquire about the job, she discovered it had been given to someone else.

At this time, there were two factions fighting for dominance in Constantinople…the Blues and the Greens. They were the equivalent of sporting clubs who were involved with the dominant sport of the day, chariot racing. When Theodora's mother took her children to the Hippodrome, where the chariot races were held, and asked the Greens for help, they laughed at her, but the Blue's gave the father employment. Theodora was to remember this humiliation for as long as she lived.

Comito, who had been born in the Hippodrome, found work there as an actress when she was around sixteen and her sister, Theodora, worked as her dresser. She eventually got minor parts in these plays and demonstrated

52

an ability to please the crowd by making strange faces and wildly obscene gestures, which pleased the crowds immensely.

When Theodora grew up, she became an extraordinarily beautiful woman, with a gorgeous figure, large eyes, and a clear, ivory complexion. She was also charming and vivacious. Even the historian Procopius, who hated her, wrote, "To express her charm in words or to embody it in a statue would be, for a mere human being, altogether impossible." Procopius also described her as "fair of face and in general attractive in appearance." She also had, it turns out, a wonderful gift for comedy...she was witty and had a superb sense of timing.

Theodora's Wild Years

She became a celebrated strip tease artist, who stripped with such flair and indecency that she became the toast of Constantinople. She had, it seems, no inhibitions or scruples and she was very imaginative and creative in finding ways to excite the crowds that came to see her. One of her most famous stunts was a parody of Leda and the Swan. This parody involved her lying on her back, with hardly anything on, while a goose pecked at some grains of corn that she hid between her legs. She rolled around the stage, exhibiting herself and pretending to have an orgasm.

Theodora also became a successful courtesan and is alleged to have held orgiastic supper parties in which her exploits were the talk of Constantinople. Procopius, who despised her and no doubt exaggerated things, described her as follows:

> She was extremely clever, and had a biting wit, and she soon became popular as a result. There was not a scrap of modesty about her, and no one ever saw her embarrassed; she would do the most shameless things without the smallest hesitation, being the sort of girl who, if you slapped her bottom or boxed her ears, would make a joke of it and roar with laughter: and she would strip herself naked and exhibit bare those parts of her body, both

before and behind, which are properly hidden from men's eyes, and should be so. She used to titillate her lovers by keeping them in suspense, and by constantly toying with new ways of making love she never failed to capture the interest of the lecherous; nor did she wait for men to accost her, but she took the initiative herself by wiggling her hips to attract their attention and by cracking suggestive jokes to all who came her way, especially if they were still in their teens. No one has ever been such a total slave to sexual pleasure and indeed to all forms of pleasure as she was. Often she would go to a party with ten young men, all of whom were at the height of their physical powers and devoted to a life of sexual indulgence, and she would sleep with every one of them, one after the other, throughout the night; then, when she had exhausted all of them, she would proceed to seduce their servants, even if there were as many as thirty, lying with each of them in turn; yet even so she would end the night unsatisfied…Moreover, although she pressed into service three entrances into her body, she often complained that nature had not made the openings in her nipples larger so that she could have invented a new way of making love there too. Naturally, she often became pregnant, but nearly always she managed to have an abortion.

There is good reason to suspect that Procopius's description of Theodora in his *Secret History* was wildly exaggerated and sensationalistic, but there seems no question that Theodora was a libertine and had an extremely active sex life. She had an illegitimate daughter when she was eighteen and is alleged to have had a son several years earlier. Procopius accused her of being a devil that had taken human form.

When she was twenty years old, she disappeared from Constantinople and reappeared in Pentapolis with a new lover, Hecebolus. She soon quarreled with him and he threw her out of his house. She eventually made her way back to Byzantium, surviving, it is thought, by becoming a prostitute.

A Meeting That Changed History

Theodora took a trip to Alexandria, where, by chance, she met Justinian…a plumpish man with a round face and curly hair who happened to be the nephew of the Emperor Justin and, as such, heir to the Roman Empire. Justin was very intelligent and was well educated. He is reputed to have lived simply and frugally. Then he met Theodora and fell madly in love with her from the moment that he first saw her. How she felt about him is unknown, but there is reason to believe she loved him and according to historical records, as far as we know, she remained faithful to him.

A short while after meeting him, she became his mistress and moved in with him. Her relationship with Justinian was complicated by two things: the fact that his uncle Justin's consort, Empress Euphemia, was against the idea of Justinian marrying Theodora and a law that prevented anyone from marrying anyone who had ever been on the stage. By a stroke of good luck, Euphemia died shortly after Justinian became involved with Theodora, so that was one roadblock out of the way. Justinian then persuaded his uncle to modify the law about marrying anyone who had been on the stage.

Justinian married Theodora shortly thereafter, in 524 A.D. The two complemented one another beautifully. She was very practical and tough minded, with an astute sense of political possibilities; he was a visionary and a dreamer, who fantasized about restoring Rome to its former glory. During their many years together, they ruled as partners and accomplished many important things. Justinian is known to have relied on Theodora for advice and her counsel was generally very good, since she was a brilliant woman and a realist. On June 28th, in 548 A.D.…at around the age of 48 (we can't be sure exactly when she was born)…she died of cancer.

Theodora's Reputation

Theodora was no saint, but we can't know how much she has become the victim of historians who have exaggerated her vices and minimized her virtues. There is also the question of how we are to judge a person who was, for a period of her life, dissolute and then, for the rest of her life, exemplary in her behavior. This is a problem that has plagued many political figures from her day to the present.

How could Theodora, portrayed by Procopius in his *Secret History*, as a nymphomaniac, as a sexual athlete of incredible powers, as a woman of awesome sexual appetites, suddenly become a loyal wife? There is good reason to suggest that Procopius was exaggerating wildly in his description of Theodora's sexual behavior? Historians have been known to "color" facts to suit their beliefs and attitudes.

One thing that Theodora's life proves is that a beautiful woman, with a good sense of humor and a native intelligence, with charm and with a talent of seizing opportunity when it presents itself, can rise in the world. Theodora was not the first woman to use her seductive beauty to find a place for herself in history. And her rise from a humble birth to become Empress is a paradigmatic story and a good example of a fact that has given hope to countless other beautiful women, who are born poor or from middling circumstances but who dream of fame and fortune and sometimes achieve it.

CHAPTER 7

LUCREZIA BORGIA: A SEDUCTRESS FROM A NICE FAMILY

Lucrezia Borgia came from a distinguished—and notorious—family, which produced two popes, Calixtus III and Alexander VI, and a famous military leader, Cesare Borgia. The Borgias originally came from a town in Spain, near Valencia, where the family name was Borja. They were members of the nobility. Alfonso Borgia was elected Pope and took the name Calixtus III. He arranged to have his nephew, Rodrigo, come to Rome.

A Nice Family
Rodrigo Borgia became a Cardinal in 1492 at the age of 25 and later became a pope. It was alleged that he purchased, so to speak, his position as pope at the cost of 150,000 ducats in payments to some Cardinals and promises of benefits to come to other Cardinals. Lucrezia Borgia was his illegitimate daughter—but only one of six illegitimate children he fathered. Three were by Lucrezia's mother Vannozza Catanei: Giovanni, Cesare and Lucrezia. Rodrigo's other three children were from assorted other mistresses.

Lucretia's First Marriage
She was raised like most wealthy children of her day and spoke Spanish, Italian, French, Greek and a smattering Latin. But her role was to be that of most women of her class and status—to be married off (to form useful political alliances) and to have children. She was not a great beauty, but she was attractive and had a certain vivacity that many people noticed.

Lucretia was married three times, and used essentially as a tool to promote her father's political ambitions. Her first marriage, in 1493, to

Giovanni Sforza, was annulled after four years. He hardly spent any time with her and the two never got on very well. This was not unusual, for like many arranged marriages, the two participants hardly knew each other and often were mismatched.

It was alleged that the Pope annulled her marriage because he wanted her for himself! The Church declared her a virga intacta, but there were many rumors that circulated in Rome about her having sexual relations with her father and both of her brothers. This led to people calling her a "second Messalina." It was thought that a little boy who was living in Cesare's court and who supposedly was Cesare's child was really Lucrezia's and that Pope Alexander VI, her father, was the father.

The Orgies.

There were numerous accounts of orgiastic parties in which Alexander VI, Rodrigo and Lucrezia, and large numbers of prostitutes, took part. According the reports, Lucrezia sat between brother and her father and presided at the orgies; she even selected the prizes that were to be awarded to the "winners." Alexander VI liked to watch young girls dancing. He also liked to lure young girls into his bed, but in that he was no different from his many Cardinals.

A very discreet letter written by Pope Pius II to Rodrigo, then a Cardinal, on June 11, 1460 offers us a sense of what went on at these orgies:

Dear Son:

We have learned that your Worthiness, forgetful of the high office with which you are invested, was present from the seventeenth to the twenty-second hour, four days ago, in the gardens of Giovanni de Bichis, where there were several women of Siena, women wholly given over to worldly vanities…We have heard that the dance was indulged in all wantonness; none of the allurements of love were lacking, and you conducted yourself in a wholly worldly manner. Shame forbids mention of all that took place…We leave it to you whether it is becoming to your dignity to court young women, and to send those whom you love fruits and wine, and during the whole day to give no thought of anything but sensual pleasure.

This letter offers us a sense of what Lucretia's father, Rodrigo, was like. But we must remember that she also participated in many of these events.

Lucretia's Second and Third Marriages

Her second marriage was to Alfonso de Bisceglie. In the early years of their marriage, she formed a small literary court, with some well-known poets in it. In 1499 she had a child while married to Bisceglie, whom she named—in honor of her father and maybe its father—Rodrigo. The marriage ended when her husband was murdered on orders of her brother Cesare Borgia, with whom she was then allegedly sleeping. Some historians believe she was also involved in the matter and either poisoned Alfonso by herself or helped poison him. Others have suggested he was strangled on orders of Cesare Borgia. This latter story is probably closer to the truth, because according to some historical accounts Alfonso did not die from poison.

After her second marriage, the Pope decided to arrange another marriage for her. She refused. When asked why she is reputed to have said "Because my husbands have been very unlucky," showing that she was, whatever else she might have been, a master of the understatement.

Her third marriage was to Alfonso d'Este, son of the Duke of Este, in 1501, and was arranged because the pope wanted to secure an alliance with the oldest and one of the most prestigious ruling houses in Italy. It was said that the only way Ercole d'Este, Alfonso's father, could get his son to agree to marry Lucrezia was to threaten to marry her himself if Alfonso wouldn't do so.

Rachel Erlanger describes how Lucrezia looked when she was to have her first meeting with her new in-laws: (1978:169)

Leaning upon the arm of an elderly cavalier dressed in black velvet she descended the steps of her palace as far as the entrance.

Over her gold-embroidered white dress with its tight barred sleeves she wore a robe of dark brown velvet lines with sable. A ruby "of no great size nor of very fine color" hung from the string of pearls about her neck. The headdress of green gauze that completed her costume was held in place by a band of beaten gold which crossed with another band edged in pearls. After the introductions and greetings were over, she ordered refreshments served and distributed small gifts of jewelry.

It must have been a rather dazzling sight. Someone at the party wrote to the duke and described her as "exceedingly gracious, most intelligent, most lovable" and added "her character is such that it is impossible to suspect anything sinister in her."

Lucrezia became a patroness of the arts and assembled a brilliant group of artists and writers around her court. This group included the painter Titian and the poet Ariosto. She also met and later had a correspondence with a poet, Pietro Bembo. This correspondence is very tender and suggests they probably loved one another.

She had three children by Alfonso in little more than two and a half years. The burden of bearing these children weakened her greatly and she died June 23, 1519. A Neapolitan poet, Giovanni Pontano, composed a scurrilous poem about her that has helped strengthen her reputation as a sinful woman:

> *Hic jacet in tumolo, Lucretia nomine sed re*
>
> *Thais. Alexandri filia, sposa, urus.*
>
> Here lies in her tomb a Lucretia in name,
>
> but a Thais in fact. Daughter, wife and daughter-in law
>
> of Alexander VI.

The Most Depraved Woman in History?

How, then, did she develop her reputation as "the most depraved woman in history?" It was rumored, as I mentioned earlier, that she had an incestuous relationship with her father, Pope Alexander VI and with her brothers Giovanni, who was murdered in 1497, and Cesare. She was alleged to have a ring with a pointy tip on it that she dipped in arsenic and used to kill her lovers when she tired of them or was ordered to do so by her father or brother for political reasons. Her father, Pope Alexander VI is supposed to have been poisoned when a servant mistakenly gave him a cup of poison that was meant for a guest that Alexander wanted to get rid of.

In judging Lucrezia Borgia, like many of the other women in this book, we must keep in mind that there are conflicting characterizations of her. She was, evidence suggests, treated like a pawn of her father and her family, and married off three times to men she didn't love. But it was not unusual for marriages to be arranged in her day and generally speaking both partners found ways of satisfying their sexual needs outside the marriage bed. In that respect, then, she was not unusual. If she actually did, as rumored, obtain her sexual gratifications from her father and her two brothers, then her reputation as a decadent woman is well deserved. But we can't be sure that these rumors were true.

So the question remains—was Lucrezia Borgia a villainess or a victim? Or was she—as is most likely—both? Her reputation as an "evil woman" is based, no doubt, on exaggerations and lies told by those who hated Pope Alexander VI and her family and saw them as part of a "Catalan plague" that had been loosed on Rome and the papacy.

There were a lot of nasty types in Rome during her day—one of the nastiest being her brother, Cesare. There is probably an element of truth in Lucretia Borgia's reputation for depravity. It would be remarkable, considering her circumstances, for her not to have some of the depravity that was all around her in Rome and so conspicuously displayed in her family rub off on her. How much rubbed off and how much was due to some natural inclination towards depravity is the question.

CHAPTER 8

MADAME DE POMPADOUR: A COLORFUL SEDUCTRESS

Jeanne-Antoinette Poisson, who became the infamous French courtesan, Madame de Pompadour, is one of the most famous of the world's great seductresses. She decided to become the mistress of Louis XV and succeeded brilliantly. She knew that the king was estranged from his wife Marie Leczinska and that he was unhappy about the death of his favorite mistress. Restless and bored, he spent a good deal of time hunting in the Forest of Senart.

A Seductress Plans a Campaign

Poisson followed his hunts in brilliantly colored carriages. She would wear a light blue costume and ride in a pink carriage one day and wear a pink costume and ride in a blue carriage the next. She also wore beautiful colorful clothes to the theater, to attract the attention of the king. At a masked ball, that celebrated the marriage of the dauphin, she met King Louis and led him to her bed. In 1745 the king gave her the title Madame de Pompadour and for twenty years, until she died in 1764, she functioned as the de facto Queen of France. Poisson, we may say, netted her man with ruthless efficiency.

There are conflicting views about her beauty. She was celebrated, in her time, as being a great beauty, but the portraits of her by various artists reveal an ordinary looking woman with a round face, even features, a clear and dazzling complexion and brilliant, sparkling eyes. She chose fabrics that complemented her complexion and her eyes. She created what we would now call a "glamorous" look.

Techniques of the Courtesans

In Ruth P. Rubinstein's *Dress Codes: Meanings and Messages in American Culture,* from which I've drawn my material on Madame de Pompadour, there is an interesting discussion of courtesans. She discusses the way they dressed and acted: (1995:115)

> The courtesans set out to look sensual. They decorated their clothing with dainty bows, ribbons, and frills. Trimmed with lace, their dresses emphasized their bosoms. Frivolity and light-heartedness characterized their appearance. Their attire glistened; it was soft and encouraged touch....
>
> The courtesans sexualized sensuality. They reddened their cheeks and nails to stimulate passion and widened the pupils of their eyes with atropine, simulating sexual excitement. They were reputed to have raised interaction with men in general, and sexual intercourse in particular, to an art. They acquired the reputation that they were beautiful, talented, imaginative, and fun to be with. They were identified as "*les grandes horizontales*" [the great horizontal ones].

This discussion offers several techniques used by the courtesans to be successful seductresses and then to keep the men they seduced. A courtesan is a woman whose profession is sex, love and romance and whose clients, generally speaking, are persons of consequence.

Courtesans can be differentiated from mistresses and prostitutes. As J. Richardson explains, (quoted in *Dress Codes,* p.115) "She is less than a mistress because she sells her love for material benefits; she is more than a prostitute because she chooses her lovers. The courtesan is a woman whose profession is love..."

Lessons in the Art of Seduction

What do we learn from these 18th Century professionals about the art of seduction?

First, we see the degree to which clothing can be used by women to arouse sexual desire in men. We all know that clothing can be used to arouse desire in men, but Madame de Pompadour made use of its powers brilliantly. In her case it was done by her attention to the colors of the clothing that she wore and the creation of a harmonious look.

The choice of fabrics is also important; some fabrics, due to their sheen and texture, emphasize the contours of a woman's body, especially a woman's bosom. Other fabrics cry out to be touched. So it isn't only the style of the clothing that counts—texture is also important.

Rubinstein points out that each culture has its own ideas about what seductive clothing is. She writes (1995:103) "each culture develops its own definitions of attire that provokes sexual interest: those who wear such attire within that cultural milieu will be seen as inviting onlookers to engage them sexually. Alluding to the body beneath it, seductive clothing is part of sexual foreplay." This is an important point, for Rubinstein is suggesting that there are no universally accepted notions of what seductive clothing is like. In some cultures a bare neck might be sexually exciting for males while in others, cleavage and exposed legs might be a powerful turn on. In actuality, since all parts of a woman's body can be covered or revealed, they all can serve as means of provoking sexual excitement in men.

Second, we see that seduction is, in some cases, something like a military campaign; it may take a long time to attract the attention of the intended seductee, stimulate his desire, and lure him into a sexual dalliance. The seductress is, in some cases, a very determined and calculating woman.

For example, in dilating (that is, enlarging) their pupils, they created a look of sexual excitement on their faces. Men, without knowing why they feel the way they do, see pictures of women with enlarged pupils as being sexually stimulating. In other cases, of course, a seduction may be something that takes place by chance, because opportunity knocks, so to speak.

Finally, there is the matter of glamour. Glamour is a rather vague term that suggests things like excitement, beauty, mystery, allure, and an exotic quality.

Thus, a woman may not be beautiful—in terms of her facial features, according to the conventions of the day—but she may possess glamour, that "something special" that makes a woman interesting, intriguing, and desirable.

The English critic John Berger suggests that glamour is always based on envy. He writes in *Ways of Seeing*, "Glamour cannot exist without personal social envy being a common and widespread emotion." (1972:148) People are caught, Berger adds, in industrial societies in which they feel powerless to achieve their desires for happiness. They are forced either to participate in a political struggle that will entail the overthrow of capitalism or to live in a state of constant envy, that takes the form of recurrent day-dreams. Advertising feeds upon this envy and "turns consumption into a substitute for democracy."

This view has implications for relations between the sexes and, of particular interest, for the way women are portrayed in paintings, advertisements, and the media. A man's presence, he says, is based on his power; a woman's presence is based on her attitude about herself and is manifested in things like her gestures, opinions, voice, clothes, and taste. Thus, there are major differences between the sexes: (1972:47)

> ...*men act* and *women appear*. Men look at women. Women watch themselves being looked at. This determines not only most relations between men and women but also the relations of women to themselves. The surveyor of woman in herself is male: the surveyed female. Thus she turns herself into an object—and most particularly an object of vision: a sight.

It is this fact, that women are visions that men continually examine (in feminist jargon, "the male gaze") that enable seductresses to turn things to their own advantage. But what about other women?

A Final Irony

Louis XV was bored; he had a wife he didn't like and his favorite mistress had just died. Thus he spent a good deal of time hunting in a forest where, it turns out, the hunter became the hunted—by the woman who was to become Madame de Pompadour. And she is a good model, though her techniques are those of the 18th Century and thus dated, for modern seductresses.

One irony of the sexual liberation of women is that sexually free women have created, it seems, the sexually bored male. Whether it is because men feel that they have lost their status as instigators of sexual activity (one traditional way of defining the male) or because they feel that they now have to perform in bed, there seems to be a strange situation in which men have become more sexually apathetic in recent years.

Could the triumph of the seductress be the male who has lost interest, who has become fat and settled down (like Emma Bovary's husband) and more interested in eating and watching television than in sexual relations with his wife, mistress, whomever? Could it be that this sexual apathy on the part of males is what is driving women to become seductresses—as often as not of their own husbands? The ubiquitous images of voluptuous women, in various stages of undress and exposure, in television commercials, magazine advertisements, films, and so on, may be over-stimulating men sexually and leading them to turn off. Seductresses may, it turns out, be their own worst enemies!

CHAPTER 9

CATHERINE THE GREAT: A LEGENDARY SEDUCTRESS

Catherine the Great was one of the most remarkable women of the modern era, whose life has become the subject of any number of legends, some true and some false...and some not only false but even ridiculous. We know a great deal about her from her memoirs and her letters and from the writings of numerous historians of her time and of recent years. By any account, her life was memorable.

Catherine's Early Years

She was born Sophia Augusta Fredericka in 1729 in Stettin, which, at that time, was under Swedish control—though since World War II it has been part of Poland. As she grew older, she developed into a very beautiful young woman. She was invited to Russia by the Empress of Russia, Elizabeth, and, after various intrigues, was married to Grand Duke Peter of Russia. She converted to the Russian Orthodox religion and learned Russian.

She was only 15 she married Peter, who was sickly all through his life and has been characterized as a weakling and perhaps even dim-witted. That was on August 21, 1745. It was, so it seems, a match made more for political reasons than due to love and passion. She didn't love him and he paid relatively little attention to her. She later suggested that she didn't have sex with him during the first five years of their marriage...and perhaps never had sex with him. There is some question about whether Peter was actually capable of having sex with a woman.

Peter's inadequacies and lack of interest led Catherine into various dalliances. There was also a need to produce an heir to the throne; if Peter couldn't do so, someone else had to be found. Their relationship makes it possible to understand why she was willing to depose him. Eighteen years after marrying Peter she engineered a coup and became Empress of Russia, which she ruled for 34 years—from 1762 to 1796. During that period she strengthened Russia, enlarged its borders, and achieved numerous reforms, but her political accomplishments have always been overshadowed in the public mind, that is, by her legendary sexuality.

Legendary Aspects of Catherine's Sexuality

It is Catherine's sexuality that is of most concern to us in this study of the seductress. She had a parade of sexual partners over the course of her career and seems to have had several long-lasting and serious love affairs, also—such as the one she had with Grigorii Potemkin.

We are fortunate in having Catherine's own assessment of the power of sexuality in human affairs. In one of her numerous love letters she writes:

> I have just said that I was pleasing, consequently half the road of temptation was already traversed, and it is the very essence of human nature that, in such cases, the other half should not remain untracked. For to tempt, and to be tempted, are things very nearly allied, and in spite of the finest maxims of morality impressed upon the mind, whenever feeling has anything to do in the matter, no sooner is it excited than we have already gone vastly father than we are aware of, and I have yet to learn how it is possible to prevent its being excited. Flight alone is, perhaps, the only remedy; but there are cases and circumstances in which flight becomes impossible, for how it is possible to fly, shun, or turn one's back in the midst of a court? The very attempt would give rise to remarks. Now, if you do not fly, there is nothing, it seems to me, so difficult to escape from that which is essentially agreeable. All that can be said in opposition to it will appear but a prudery quite out of harmony with the natural instincts of the

human heart; besides, no one holds his heart in his hand, tightening or relaxing his grasp of its pleasure.

This letter expresses an extremely interesting theory of human sexuality. She starts by noting that she was physically attractive and that being attractive is an important element in being a temptress. The second point she makes is that there is a relationship of significance, generally disregarded, between tempting and being tempted, due to the power of sexuality and our capacity for becoming sexually excited. A temptress "needs" someone willing—and perhaps wanting—to be tempted. There is also the matter of human nature.

We become a prisoner, she suggests, of our natural instincts and inclinations towards gratification. That is, we cannot rationally deal with our physical desires; only flight and distance might help, but flight is impossible to someone who must be at the court all the time.

Catherine dealt with her need to satisfy her sexual desires by separating her sexual life from her role as Empress of Russia and by adopting a policy of having a succession of lovers. This would prevent her from becoming dominated by one, but the cost was that she never was able to have a long-term and satisfying love relationship. Her real passion was politics so her problems with men may not have been as significant as one might imagine.

Her promiscuity reached legendary dimensions, even in her own time. She had, it seems, a predilection for young Russian men. A former envoy to her court from England, Sir George Macartney, explained why she preferred Russian men with a curious and rather fantastic theory:

> It is evident from lists given of the Empresses [sic] Favourites that she has always of late preferred a Russian to one of any other Nation. This may be partly owing to a fear of exciting any jealousy in the Nation, but by some is attributed to an idea that the Russians excel even the Irish in a certain *Manly* accomplishment, or rather features of their Persons. The Russian Nurses it is said make a constant practice of pulling it, when the child is young,

which has a great effect of lengthening the *virile instrument*. It is very certain that pulling and stroking the note lengthens and raises it much and a similar plan may be some effect on other parts of the body.

Most of Catherine's lovers were young officers of her Guards. Since this unit played a major role in maintaining her rule, there may have been political as well as sexual reasons for her choice of these men.

There is also a myth that Catherine has several "testers" who slept with men and gave her reports about their sexual proficiency. Thus, a certain Countess Bruce in Catherine's court was held to be Catherine's "eprouveuse" or tester of male capacity. Once a person gains a reputation for something, embellishments are easy to create, so stories about Catherine multiplied.

In actuality, it has been estimated that she had no more than ten or twelve lovers during her 34 years on the throne, which suggests that legends about her being an insatiable nymphomaniac are quite ridiculous. It is true that she had a considerable number of liaisons with lovers, but that is not the same thing as being a nymphomaniac. (We do the same thing in America and elsewhere nowadays but formalize our relationships by what has been called "serial monogamy." It is far from unusual to meet people who have been married four or five times and some poor creatures have been married ten or twelve times.)

The Bestiality Myth

According to the bestiality myth, Catherine died by "penile impalement" when a horse that she was about to have sex with, fell on her. In another version, the horse was lowered on her too quickly. It is not known when this story started circulating, but large numbers of people have thought it was correct, and still do, to this day. It is part of folklore about Catherine and, as such, is impossible to kill. The story suggests that Catherine's desire for sexual experience knew no bounds and that even

Russians, with their supposedly elongated penises (according to Macartney's bizarre theory) were not enough for her.

In actuality, Catherine died on November 5, 1796 in her Palace. Her chamberlain found her on the floor in one of her closets. It took six men to carry her to her bed—for she had become very fat. Doctors were summoned but it was impossible to save her. In the afternoon she was given communion and last rites. She had died, an autopsy revealed, of a cerebral stroke. She was 67 years old.

The most common myth about Catherine is that on any given evening, being a creature of insatiable sexual hunger, she would typically have sexual intercourse with a huge number of her guards, one after another. Given that fantastic notion, it is not too difficult to understand why the myth of Catherine dying by having a horse fall on her would be seen as credible.

The "Problem" of Catherine

Catherine is said to have written, "my heart cannot willingly remain one hour without love." This would suggest a woman dominated by passion, which would explain her sexual exploits— but that was not the case at all. She was also, historians generally agree, a political genius who ran Russia for 34 years and who helped restore Russia to its former glory. She reformed the Russian military system and economy and practiced a forwarded looking foreign policy. She wrote a great deal and corresponded with Voltaire and Diderot in France, among others. She also is reputed to have been a brilliant conversationalist. Most of her energy went into running the country.

Catherine's complexity raises the question of how we are to make sense of her behavior. We have what seems to be a classic example of compartmentalization—a term also used to describe Bill Clinton's capacity to run the government while being impeached by the Congress for his "bimbo eruptions" and sexual transgressions. It seems that Catherine was able to prevent her private passions and personal life from impinging, in any significant way, on her public life, as a monarch.

What has happened, of course, is that history has tended to neglect her political achievements and focus attention, for the most part, on her sexual improprieties. In part this is because history is written mostly by male historians, whose sense of morality, whose anxieties (about "devouring" females), and maybe whose fantasies, are responsible for the picture we have of Catherine. Her image, like many of the other seductresses discussed in this book, is one that has been given to us mostly by men. We must keep that in mind all the time.

The Gorer Swaddling Hypothesis and Catherine's Hypersexuality

As a footnote to this study of Catherine, let me mention a fascinating and probably preposterous theory about Russian character and culture that was put forward by the British anthropologist Geoffrey Gorer. Catherine, we must remember, was a German princess, but from the age of fifteen until her death she lived in Russia and might well have been influenced by Russian culture.

Gorer's thesis, as elaborated in his book *The People of Great Russia: A Psychological Study*, is that the custom of swaddling infants from working class families in Greater Russia had profound effects upon their character and Russian culture. He explains that swaddling involves wrapping a baby in long strips of material that hold its legs strait and ties its arm by its sides. When swaddled, a baby is completely rigid. This swaddling is typically done for the first nine months of a baby's life. Official policy tried to dissuade people from swaddling babies but except for children of the intelligentsia, most babies in Greater Russia were swaddled.

Gorer deduces (and he takes pains to say that he is making deductions) that the babies responded to their swaddling and immobility with "intense and destructive rage" that was directed at the swaddling. As he writes (1962:126) "it would seem that infants sometimes exhaust themselves physically and psychologically with unassuaged rage." This leads, ultimately, to the Russians not having internalized ethical restraints to guide their conduct. Their early experience of being tightly controlled and then being given freedom leads to a Russian personality that alternates between orgiastic feasts and sexual license and an unconscious search for total absolution. As Gorer explains: (1962:139):

What Russians value are not minimum gratifications—enough to get along with—but maximum total gratifications—orgiastic feasts, prolonged drinking bouts, high frequency of copulation, and so on.

This mindset, which according to Gorer's theory would be that of the people she ruled and many of the people around her, in her court, might help explain, in part, Catherine's behavior and the willingness of so many of the members of her court to have sexual relationships with her.

CHAPTER 10

MATA HARI: THE SPY SEDUCTRESS

On March 13, 1905 Mata Hari gave an eagerly awaited performance in the Musee Guimet. She performed as a Hindu dancer. She was half-naked and danced slowly and sensuously. She wore a golden collar around her throat and carried a number of veils that she flung about her. After her dance, she explained, in French:

> My dance is a sacred poem in which each movement is a word and whose every word is underlined by music. The temple in which I dance can be vague or faithfully reproduced, as here today. For I am the temple.

After her short lecture, the translated it into English, German, Dutch and Javanese. She became the toast of Paris.

The French newspapers gave readers her biography. She was, they wrote, Indian and came from a distinguished Brahmin family. Her mother died while giving birth to her. She was adopted and was raised by priests who gave her the name Mata Hari. She was cloistered in their temples until a high priestess consecrated her to Shiva's service.

Mata Hari added to the story. "It was on the purple granite altar of Kanda Swamy that, at the age of thirteen, I danced for the first time, completely nude." The story was complete nonsense. Mata Hari was born as Margarethta Geertruida Zelle, had married a military officer from the Dutch East Indies, Rudolph MacLeod, who she met when he was home on leave. She was eighteen and he was forty. But all that was in the distant past. She was now Mata Hari, exotic dancer.

A typical newspaper description of her went as follows:

Tall and slender, she carried a marvelous neck, supple and the color of amber, a fascinating face that makes a perfect oval and whose sybilline and tempting expression strikes everyone at first sight. The mouth firmly outlined, traces a mobile line, disdainful, very alluring, under a nose, straight and fine, the nostrils of which quiver above two shadowy dimples. Her magnificent eyes, velvety and dark, and slightly slanting and set with long curving lashes—they are enigmatic, seeming to look into the beyond. Her black hair, divided in two bands, makes for her face a dark and wavy frame. The effect is voluptuous, possessing a magic beauty and an astonishing purity of outline...

She danced a number of times at the Trocadero Theater and at other theaters in Paris and was wildly popular. Her success in Paris led to her traveling all through Europe to give performances and she was to spend the next ten years dancing.

That led to a period of libertine activity in which she had affairs with many famous men. Erika Ostrovky describes her in *Eye of Dawn: The Rise and Fall of Mata Hari:* (1978:93)

She flitted from man to man—ambassadors, diplomats, bankers, aristocrats, politicians, industrialists, composers, impresarios, journalists—partly out of restlessness, partly because she always remembered that the *Kamasutra* taught:

The duty of the courtesan consists in having affairs with the right men, to obtain the wealth of the men involved with her, and to get rid of them after having despoiled them of their riches.

Perfidiousness was obviously part of the game and only added to one's attractiveness. Men were drawn like night moths to such a consuming flame.

She was considered to be "the costliest delicacy on the continental menu."

By 1913, however, she noticed that she was beginning to show her age and people were turning their attention elsewhere. Her last public performance was in 1914 in the Hague, where her performance was given a lukewarm response.

In truth, she was not much of a dancer, but had a distinct talent for taking off her clothes and displaying herself. A famous ballerina is reputed to have said about her, "She is as much an Indian dancer as I am a Chinese waiter." It was her celebrity status that enabled her to build a career as a dancer and then a courtesan. And it was her desire for excitement, it would seem, that led her to become a German spy.

The Spy

When she was around forty, she became a German agent, having been trained in a German spy academy in Antwerp under the tutelage of a legendary spymaster, Fräulein Doktor also known as the Red Tiger. This training lasted fifteen weeks. Mata Hari had become agent H21. Fräulein Doktor is alleged to have cautioned Mata Hari about being aware of her pride and about the danger of either failing or betraying her new masters.

She returned to Paris, where, for a number of reasons, the French and British spy services became suspicious of her behavior and had placed her under close observation. She had been overheard speaking perfect German while traveling on a German ship. Other things she did were troubling. After rounding up information about her over a period of months, the French and British espionage bureaus concluded that she was a spy

Later on, having broken the German codes, they intercepted messages from a German military attaché named Kalle, in Madrid, about an agent H21 who it was obvious had to be Mata Hari:

Give H21 3,000 francs and tell her/him that:

1. The results obtained are not satisfactory.

2. The ink which H21 received cannot be developed by the French if the correspondence paper is treated in conformity with instructions before and after the use of invisible ink.

3. If, in spite of that, H21 does not want to work with invisible ink, the agent should come to Switzerland and, from there, communicate her/his address to A.

The French secret service collected any number of other messages about H21. She was later "recruited" to be a double agent for the French, but they were not sure that she could be trusted. It is also possible that the Germans, somehow, found out that Mata Hari had become a double agent.

According to Russell Warren Howe, author of *Mata Hari: The True Story*, the Germans intended to have their messages about her decoded, because they wanted the French to arrest her and execute her, because they were convinced she was not useful to them. As he explains: (1986:143)

> ...all Kalle's messages and Berlin responses were in the old code that the British had broken earlier and that the Germans knew that the Allies possessed. *They were therefore meant to be read by the French*...The whole traffic between Madrid and Berlin about "H21"—who clearly is Mata Hari—was therefore a gigantic bluff to persuade the French to arrest their probationer-spy and shoot her.

Mata Hari, however, didn't have the slightest notion that she was under suspicion of being a spy. She was eventually arrested, tried and found guilty of being a spy for the Germans. She was executed on October 16, 1917. Mata Hari's story ends rather pathetically; she wasn't even given the dignity of a burial. Her cadaver was given to students in a French medical school.

The Myth of Mata Hari

Julia Keay in *The Spy Who Never Was: The Life and Loves of Mata Hari* argues that her death sentence was completely unjustified. She writes: (1987:208, 209)

For more than forty years no one was prepared to admit that her trial was a travesty of justice and that Mata Hari had been sacrificed to official expediency—and by then there were few who cared. Yet there has always been something fascinating about the combination of beauty and wickedness, and black as the French Government tried to paint her, it was the glamour rather than the infamy of her story that caught the public eye.

Keay mentions that there were wild rumors that she hadn't be killed—that a lover had bribed the firing squad to load their rifles with blank bullets and then rode a horse into the area where she was to be shot, swooped her up and carried her off. Another rumor was that she wore nothing but a fur coat to her execution and just before she was to be shot, she took off her coat and the members of the firing squad, excited by seeing her naked body, missed her when they shot at her. There were rumors of people seeing her ten years after she was supposed to have been executed.

She is alleged to have been responsible for mutinies in the French army, for the deaths of 50,000 French soldiers, and for the success of a German submarine campaign against Allied shipping, among other things. As Keay concludes, "Every person who had been present at her trial…and every official who had been involved in the preparation of the case against her seized the chance to justify his actions and enhance his own reputation by painting her as the very incarnation of evil." (1987: 208)

This legendary figure was portrayed in films by three actresses who are legendary in their own right—Greta Garbo played her in the film *Mata Hari*, Marlene Dietrich in a take-off of the Mata Hari legend, *Dishonored*, and Jean Moreau in *Mata Hari, Agent H-21*. Mata Hari has also become a figure of speech, as in "she's no Mata Hari.". She remains a remarkable study in self-creation and self-destruction.

CHAPTER 11

MONICA LEWINSKY: THE "INNOCENT" SEDUCTRESS

Monica Lewinsky's "seduction" of President Bill Clinton has an almost Biblical quality to it. There is relatively little in the way of elaboration. All we know is that before her involvement with the President, she had established eye contact with him, and then, on that fateful November 15th, 1997, she showed him the straps of her thong underwear. This scenario is described in the Starr Report.

The Starr Report

Let me quote from the Starr Report. It is on the Internet along with transcripts of Monica Lewinsky's infamous tapes with Linda Tripp and many other documents connected to the Lewinsky-Clinton relationship.

November 15 Sexual Encounter

According to Ms. Lewinsky, she and the President made eye contact when he came to the West Wing...At one point, Ms. Lewinsky and the President talked alone in the Chief of Staff's Office. In the course of flirting with him, she raised her jacket in the back and showed him the straps of her thong underwear, which extended above her pants. En route to the rest room at about 8:00 PM, she passed George Stepanopoulos's office. The President was inside, alone, and he beckoned her to enter. She told him that she had a crush on him. He laughed, then asked if she would like to see his private office.

That was what precipitated the affair between Clinton and Lewinsky. She had been sexually active for many years (and had an affair with a professor at the college she attended) and thus was not, in any sense, an innocent 22 year old young woman.

The Lewinsky Seduction

Her seduction of President Clinton had some of the classic elements of a seduction, but in a highly compressed manner. We see the following elements in her seduction of President Bill Clinton:

1. She is seen.

She points out that she has established "eye contact" with the President, much the way that Madame de Pompadour managed to be seen by Louis XIV. It is, after all, difficult for a woman to seduce someone if he doesn't know that you exist.

2. She flirts with the President.

The seductress must be someone who can interest and later bewitch the person she wishes to seduce. Flirting is often a beginning step in the process that leads, ultimately, to a seduction. Flirting has an element of play to it; in some cases it is an end in itself but in other cases it leads to a more intimate kind of sexual relationship.

3. She shows him the straps of her thong underwear.

Here, she indicates that she is a highly charged sexual being by showing the President the straps of her thong underwear. This suggests that she is interested in some kind of a sexual relationship and the straps are shown as a sign that other things are to come.

4. She tells him she has a "crush" on him.

The seductress entrances her potential victim with her words. Monica Lewinsky, a young woman, uses the vernacular of people of her age. Telling him that she has a crush on him suggests she is interested in having sexual relationships with him.

5. The President succumbs to the temptation of the seductress.

President Clinton invites Monica Lewinsky into his private office and the stage is sex for a sexual relationship—though not sexual intercourse. Neither President Clinton nor Monica Lewinsky defined their relationship as a sexual one. She characterized her relationships with the President as "just fooling around," not real sex. He is a baby boomer figure, caught in between an older generation who see oral sex as a sinful sexual relationship and a younger generation that sees oral sex as "just fooling around" and nothing really serious.

This relationship then precipitated a crisis in the American presidency and led to the President being impeached and his being put on trial by the Senate. The ironic situation is that the President's popularity remained very high, in part because many Americans saw the proceedings as partisan and the Republicans, who were "out to get" the President, as attempting to nullify his election.

The Lewinsky Seduction and Culture Wars in America

The relationship spawned many sexual jokes about the President and Monica Lewinsky and has become part of American folklore and jokelore. Thus, the riddle:

Q. How did Clinton violate the 11th Commandment?

R.. Answer: Thou shall not put thy rod in thy staff!

Let me offer a number of other jokes, riddles, etc. on Bill Clinton which I've taken from the Internet.

Q. What's the difference between Bill Clinton and a screwdriver ?

R.. A screwdriver turns and screws, Clinton screws 'n-turns'.

Mr. Reagan, Mr. Bush and Mr. Clinton are on the Titanic. Mr. Reagan says, "Save the Women!" Mr. Bush says, "Screw the women!" Mr. Clinton says, "Do we have Time?!"

What is Bill's idea of safe sex? When Hillary is out of town.

Once Bill Clinton visited an elementary school to talk to a group of 3rd graders. He said to them, "Today we are going to discuss the difference between a tragedy, a great loss and an accident". Then he said, "Can anyone give me an example of a tragedy?" A little boy raises his hand and says, "If a kid runs out in the street after a ball and gets hit by a car." Clinton says, "No, that would be an accident. Can anyone else try?" A little girl raises her hand and says, "If a busload of kids drove off a cliff." Clinton says, "No, that would be a great loss. Come on, anyone else?" A boy raises his hand and says and says, "If you and Mrs. Clinton was on a plane and it blew up." Then Clinton says, "Well, Yes, but can you tell me why it would be considered a tragedy?" And the little boy says, "Well, it wouldn't have been an accident, and it sure as heck wouldn't have been a great loss."

Allegedly Monica Lewinsky, in a statement released today, countered President Clinton's firm denial:

> I have had enough. This whole experience has left a bitter taste in my mouth, and I can't stomach any more. I feel as if I am getting the shaft, that this ugly matter has come to a head and blown up in my face. This may be a load to handle, but when things are hard, that is when I am at my best. I have faced hard things in the past, and I know what is coming. I will meet this challenge the only way I know: that is, head on. I have licked bigger things than this before, and I will again. No one will ever be able to say that Monica Lewinsky isn't a finisher, that she quit before the job was done. I will work non-stop and fight this, blow by blow, until I am wiped clean of this dirty affair. I will not be stained by it.
>
> Thank you.
>
> Monica Lewinsky

The Center for Disease Control in Atlanta, Georgia announced today that the President has proven that you CAN get sex from aides.

There was a survey in the US where 600 women were asked if they would sleep with Bill Clinton.
82% replied never again.

Why does Hillary want to have sex with Bill every day at 5 am?
She wants to make sure that she is the first lady.

There's a new Bill Clinton computer coming out soon. It will have a six-inch hard drive, but no memory.

Similarities between Nixon and Clinton:
Nixon: Watergate. Clinton: Waterbed.
Nixon: His biggest fear - the Cold War.
Clinton: His biggest fear - a Cold Sore.
Nixon: Worried about carpet bombs.
Clinton: Worried about carpet burns.
Nixon: Couldn't stop Kissinger.
Clinton: Couldn't stop kissing her.
Nixon: Couldn't explain the 18-minute gap in the Watergate tape.
Clinton: Couldn't explain the 36-DD bra in his brief case.
Nixon: His nickname was Tricky Dick.
Clinton: Same.
Nixon: Ex-President.
Clinton: Sex-President.
There are an endless number of other jokes, many quite poor and tasteless, that have been circulating on the Internet. These jokes have a double valence: they poke fun at the President but they also suggest that

his relationship with Monica Lewinsky is nothing particularly serious. In American culture, a sexual super-stud gains a kind of heroic quality, so Clinton emerges as an important new figure in our folklore.

Monica Lewinsky, like many of her "rock" generation, probably sees sexual activity as merely one more form of leisure activity and sex outside of marriage not as something morally repugnant. Thus, the Lewinsky-Clinton affair became part of the culture wars in which the younger generation's postmodern behavior patterns came into conflict, in a very graphic way, with the values and beliefs of an older generation and especially with that element of the population with conservative values and beliefs.

To those with a Biblical or so-called "conservative" perspective, the seductress is still a demon and involvement with her inevitably leads to death and destruction, not only of the individual but, in addition, of the society in which she functions. That is because she is seen to be like a virus that contaminates the society in which she is found.

For young people, on the other hand, seduction loses its definition as something demonic or significant and merely becomes one more technique that women can use to find sexual gratification. It isn't morality that makes most young people hesitate about casual sexual relations but fear of AIDS.

Part III:

The Seductress as Metaphor

CHAPTER 12

SEDUCTION SCENES IN MICKEY SPILLANE'S *I, THE JURY*

More than six million copies of Mickey Spillane's first detective thriller, *I, The Jury,* have been sold, making this violent and sexually titillating story one of the best selling books ever published in America. It's ending, to be discussed shortly, is also one of the most famous (or some would say infamous or notorious) resolutions of a murder mystery in American detective fiction.

The hero of this story, Mike Hammer, is a tough, vengeance-ridden private investigator who discovers that his best friend, Jack Williams, who saved Hammer's life when they were soldiers, has been brutally and sadistically murdered. Williams had lost his right arm saving Hammer's life and he vows that no matter what happens, he will find Williams' murderer and kill him. He vows "he will die exactly as you died, with a .45 slug in the gut, just below the belly button. No matter who it is, Jack, I'll get the one."

Hammer's search for the murderer leads him along many different paths and he meets a large number of people, many of whom are very attractive women. In the course of his investigation, he meets a beautiful psychiatrist, Charlotte Manning, with whom he falls in love and to whom he eventually proposes marriage. She accepts. There are a number of scenes in the book where they are kissing and where she wants to go to bed with him, but he always refuses.

In one scene, for example, he visits her and by chance (just after she has taken a shower) comes upon her standing by her bed, completely naked. She hastily puts on a robe and a short while later we find the following dialogue:

"Mike," she whispered, "I want you."

"No," I said.

"Yes. You must."

"No."

"But, Mike, why? Why?"

"No, darling, it's too beautiful to spoil. Not now. Our time will come, but it must be right."

This pattern of sexual teasing is shown throughout the book, but there are a number of times in the book when Hammer is seduced or a seduction is attempted. Hammer won't have sex with Charlotte Manning until they are married, but he does have sex, at different times, with each of the Bellamy sisters. They are gorgeous twin sisters—Mary and Esther and each of them seduces him.

In the first seduction scene, Hammer goes to interview Esther to get some information that might help him solve the murder. He goes to her house and notices that her dinner dress cunningly reveals "the lovely lines of her body." She brings drinks and Hammer asks her some questions. She crosses her legs and Mike asks himself "why don't women learn to keep their skirts low enough to keep men from thinking the wrong thing? Guess that's why they wear them short."

Esther sees that Hammer is looking at her legs and covered them up. A short while later she tilts her head back to laugh, giving Hammer a "full view of her breasts." (118) He puts his drink down on the coffee table, circles it and sits down beside Esther. We then find the following: (118, 119)

> She put her arms around my neck and pulled my mouth down close to hers....Her mouth met mine, her arms getting tighter behind me. I leaned on her heavily, letting my body caress hers. She rubbed her face against mine, breathing hotly on my neck. Whenever I touched her she trembled. She worked a hand free and I heard snaps on her dress opening. I kissed her shoulders, the tremble turned into a shudder. Once she bit me, her teeth

sinking into my neck. I held her tighter and her breathing turned into a gasp. She was squirming against me, trying to release the passion that was inside her.

My hand found the full cord on the lamp beside the divan and the place was in darkness. Just the two of us. Little sounds. No words. There wasn't need for any. A groan once or twice. The rustle of the cushions and the rasping sound of fingernails on broadcloth. The rattle of a belt buckle and the thump of a shoe kicked to the floor. Just the breathing, the wetness of a kiss.

Shortly after they have had sex, Hammer and Esther start joking about a birthmark she is supposed to have and shortly after that Hammer leaves the house.

There is very little detail about this seduction, or the one, later on in the book, in which Esther's sister, Mary Bellamy, seduces Mike. It all happens very quickly. He has become excited by seeing her body, her legs, and her breasts. Her displaying her legs is taken by him as a signal that she wants to have sex with him. And he has had something to drink. But he certainly doesn't put up much resistance—even though he is able to resist his fiancée, Charlotte Manning, any number of times.

The most celebrated seduction attempt in the book—and one of the most famous ones in American tough guy detective novels, takes place at the very end of the book. Hammer has discovered that Charlotte Manning is the person who has killed Jack Williams and confronts her. In the last eight pages of the book we find Hammer offering a long monologue, accusing Manning of the murder. Hammer says, at one point, "You no longer had the social instinct of a woman—that of being dependent upon a man." We also find, in italics, a description of Charlotte's attempt to seduce Hammer, by doing a strip-tease, as Hammer talks.

(*She was standing in front of me now. I felt a hot glow go over me as I saw what she was about to do. Her hands came up along her sides pressing her clothes tightly against her skin, then slowly ran under her breasts, cupping them. Her fingers fumbled with the buttons of her blouse, but not for long. They came open—one by one.)*

Hammer continues offering his monologue and his description of Charlotte slowly disrobing, until she is completely naked.

(Her thumbs hooked in the fragile silk of the panties and pulled them down. She stepped out of them as delicately as one coming from a bathtub. She was completely naked now. A sun-tanned goddess giving herself to her lover. With arms outstretched she walked toward me. Lightly, her tongue ran over her lips, making them glisten with passion. She smell of her was like an exhilarating perfume. Slowly, a sigh escaped her, making the hemispheres of her breasts quiver. She leaned forward to kiss me, her arms going out to encircle my neck.)

The roar of the .45 shook the room. Charlotte staggered back a step. Her eyes were a symphony of incredulity, an unbelieving witness to truth. Slowly, she looked down at the ugly swelling in her naked belly where the bullet went in.

Just before she dies, she asks him "How could you?" He replies, "it was easy." He also discovers that she had left a gun, with the safety latch off, on a table behind him. Had he kissed her, we are led to conclude, she would have killed him as cold bloodedly as she had killed Jack Williams and a number of other people.

This seduction leads to a different kind of outcome than we get in normal ones—she is penetrated by a lead bullet rather than Mike Hammer's penis, and she dies unable to accept the fact that her sexual allure had not led Hammer to succumb to her.

I, The Jury raises a number of issues that are relevant to our study of seduction. First, we can see that not all seduction attempts are successful; Charlotte Manning's striptease and everything that went with it could not prevent Mike Hammer from carrying out his vow—to avenge the murder of his friend. Quite likely a number of seduction attempts by women in real life also fail, for reasons I've discussed earlier. It is even possible that some men are too dense to realize that a woman is trying to seduce them (and the women may use techniques that are too subtle, so the seduction attempt is not recognized)!

Second, we can see that sometime seductresses have ulterior motives and that they are using their sexual appeal, not because they are in love or are carried away or desire sexual satisfaction, but for something else—even murder.

Finally, we can see that there is a considerable difference between the seduction scenes in *The Locked Room* (to be discussed in the next chapter) and *I, The Jury*. There is a difference between seduction in elite culture, as represented by Auster novel, and popular culture, as represented by the Spillane thriller.

Let me suggest, taking a few liberties and simplifying things a bit, that there are two different codes of seduction that are reflected in elite and popular culture—what might be called the restricted code and the elaborated code. The elaborated seduction code reflects the lifestyles of educated, upper-middle (and higher) class people, and is more elaborate, more subtle, more complicated and slower than the restricted seduction code. This discussion of codes is based on the two novels I have analyzed, but it probably extends to elite culture and popular culture in general.

The elaborated seduction code has complex characters, a great deal of dialogue, little description of the bodies of the women, and what might be called "intellectual" surrender. The characters drink wine and eat gourmet food. The restricted seduction code has one-dimensional characters, relatively little dialogue in the seduction scenes, a great deal of description of the bodies of the seductresses and the characters surrender due to physical desire. They drink hard liquor and there's little or no food involved in these seductions.

These two novels, *The Locked Room* and *I The Jury* are, quite probably, extreme examples; most novels, detective stories, and other narratives that have seduction scenes in them fall in between, no doubt. But they serve to highlight and emphasize the differences between seduction as it is reflected in popular culture and elite culture and as it is tied socio-economic classes in America, and perhaps elsewhere.

CHAPTER 13

JANE FANSHAWE IN THE LOCKED ROOM

Paul Auster's book, *The Locked Room.*(Penguin Books, 1986) contains a very graphic and classic portrayal of a seduction by a woman. This book, volume three of his remarkable The New York Trilogy, deals with a character named Fanshawe who is a childhood neighbor and friend of the narrator and a person he idolized. Fanshawe goes to Harvard, drops out, wanders around, does a great deal of writing, marries a beautiful woman named Sophie, with whom he has a child, and then disappears. He has instructed his wife, should something happen to him, to contact the narrator and give him his manuscripts to dispose of as he sees fit. The narrator arranges to publish Fanshawe's books, which are very successful. The narrator marries Fanshawe's wife and starts writing a biography of Fanshawe. Eventually, the narrator is shocked to discover that his identity is beginning to merge into Fanshawe's.

A Detailed Seduction Scenario

There is a seduction scene in the book of great interest, for Auster spells out how the seduction is accomplished in considerable detail. I will quote some of the relevant passages, which cover nine pages, and comment on what they reflect upon the techniques involved in seduction—as Auster describes them, that is.

The narrator has traveled to the home of Fanshawe's mother, Jane Fanshawe, to photocopy some letters she has from him. He goes off to spend a couple of hours photocopying the letters. When he returns he finds, to his surprise, that Fanshawe's mother has made an elegant lunch with white wine, cold salmon, asparagus, and cheeses. She served this on her best china in a room full of flowers. It was obvious to the narrator, from a "thickening" in her voice, that she had begun drinking earlier.

He recognizes that she may be attempting to seduce him and tells himself to "watch it," especially since they are drinking a great deal of wine. As he says, "I began to expect the worst." What is particularly interesting is the power of Mrs. Fanshawe's voice. It melts his resistance and in a strange way hypnotizes him:

> She went on like this for more than an hour, her words gradually mounting in bitterness, at some point reaching a moment of sustained clarity, and then, following the next glass of wine, gradually losing coherence. Her voice was hypnotic. As long as she went on speaking, I felt that nothing could touch me anymore. There was a sense of being immune, or being protected by the words that came from her mouth. I scarcely bothered to listen. I was floating inside that voice. I was surrounded by it, buoyed up by its persistence, going with the flow of syllables, the rise and fall, the waves.

The Power of Sunlight

He also is dazzled by the quality of light in the room. The lighting generates a kind of radiance that contributes to his falling under the spell of Mrs. Fanshawe. The butter that melts under the heat of the sun is a metaphor for his resistance that fades under the onslaught of her talk and the semi-trance he finds himself in. It is interesting that the strong sunlight is an important part of this seduction. Usually, it is dim light that casts a romantic glow on things that is found in seduction scenarios.

He is aware, in a somewhat vague manner, of what she is doing but feels powerless to help himself. The light that streams into the room gives the bottles on the table a strange radiance. He recognizes that he should not let her continue to talk, to bedazzle him, but cannot help himself. He also recalls one afternoon, when he was a young boy living next door, how he, by chance, was able to gaze upon her body and how this image had been with him for many years. The power of images and his memory of an early image are both of consequence here. The narrator is somewhat drunk, but he recognizes that his drunkenness is not enough to explain his feelings or his behavior. There's something else—he has seen, when a young and lustful teenager, Mrs. Fanshawe's breasts and much of her body and that image had stuck with him for years.

As the narrator explains, recalling events that happened when he was just thirteen or fourteen:

> There was one in particular that struck me with great force: an afternoon in August when I was thirteen or fourteen, looking through my bedroom window into the yard nest door and seeing Mrs. Fanshawe walk out in a red two-piece bathing suit, casually unhook the top half, and lie down on a lawn chair with her back to the sun. I had been sitting by my window day-dreaming, and then, unexpectedly, a beautiful woman comes sauntering into my field of vision, almost naked, unaware of my presence, as though I had conjured her myself. This image stayed with me for a long time, and I returned to it often during my adolescence....

We have a curious situation here. The narrator, in the process of being seduced, realizes what is happening and recognizes that if he doesn't use all his "strength to fight it," he would be seduced. The situation, the narrator tells us, was both natural and grotesque. Sapping his strength is the matter of memory—many years ago, when he was a young teenager, by chance he had seen Mrs. Fanshawe's breasts and the power of that image had stayed with him for many years and was even affecting him now.

The Power of Touch

And then, when the narrator goes to comfort Mrs. Fanshawe, who has broken down crying, he becomes carried away and unable to stop himself. Just touching her generates a sexual fervor and before he knows it, he is lying naked in bed with Mrs. Fanshawe and penetrating her. His being somewhat drunk, he adds, was not a valid excuse for what he did.

> It began not long after she started to cry—when she finally
> exhausted herself and the words broke apart, crumbling into tears.
> Drunk, filled with emotion, I stood up, walked over to where she
> was sitting, and put my arms around her in a gesture of comfort.
> This carried us across the threshold. Mere contact was enough to
> trigger a sexual response, a blind memory of other bodies, of other
> embraces, and a moment later we were kissing, and then, not
> many moments after that, lying naked on her bed upstairs.

Even his sense of guilt was not enough to stop him, he adds. He is able
to rationalize his behavior and convince himself that his having sex with
Mrs. Fanshawe is really trivial and of no significance to his life. This is just
a momentary fling, he tells himself, that will have no consequences.

> Although I was drunk, I was not so far gone that I didn't know
> what I was doing. But not even guilt was enough to stop me. The
> moment will end, I said to myself, and no one will be hurt. It has
> nothing to do with my life, nothing to do with Sophie. But then,
> even as it was happening, I discovered that there was more to it
> than that. For the fact was that I was fucking Fanshawe's
> mother—but in a way that had nothing to do with pleasure.

We now see that the narrator's seduction is almost one that he willed
and that it has an ulterior purpose. He has been carried away, he has been
seduced by Mrs. Fanshawe, but he find that his having sex with her is connected not with desire but with a sudden hatred he feels towards
Fanshawe, a feeling that he wants to kill Fanshawe and hurt his mother.

Dark Shadows

Here, the narrator explores the hidden reasons behind his lack of ten-
derness towards Mrs. Fanshawe. An act of love turns into an act of
vengeance and hatred:

I was fucking out of hatred, and I turned it into an act of violence, grinding away at this woman as though I wanted to pul-
verize her. I had entered my own darkness, and it was there that
I learned the one thing that is more terrible than anything else:
that sexual desire can also be the desire to kill, that a moment
comes when it is possible for a man to choose death over life.
This woman wanted me to hurt her and I did, and I found
myself reveling in my cruelty.

This seduction scene is quite remarkable in the way it deals with the
techniques of female seduction and with the complex matters and feelings
behind the narrator's sexual relationship with Mrs. Fanshawe. He fools
himself, convincing himself that his sexual dalliance with her is of no consequence, only to recognize, a short while later, that his fucking Mrs.
Fanshawe is connected with all kinds of dark shadows in his psyche. She
has told him that he looks a lot like Fanshawe, that the two of them were
like brothers, almost like twins. She also tells the narrator that her son
hated her, cringed every time she went near him.

This suggests that her seduction of the narrator has strong Oedipal
qualities and that she is a kind of Jocasta figure and he is a substitute for a
withdrawn and hateful son. Auster is open about this matter. In one passage he has his narrator speculating, "Recently, I've begun to wonder if she
didn't somehow sense a hatred in me for Fanshawe that was just as strong
as her own. Perhaps she felt this unspoken bond between us, perhaps it
was the kind of bond that could proved only through some perverse,
extravagant act. Fucking me would be like fucking Fanshawe—like fucking her own son—and in the darkness of this sin, she would have him
again—but only in order to destroy him. A terrible revenge." (p. 107)

We these considerations in mind, let us look at the techniques used in
the seduction scenario in the book.

The Art of Seduction as Reflected in The Locked Room

It is worth considering the different elements mentioned in the narrator's seduction to see what the passage reflects about technical aspects of the art of seduction by women.

Food.

There is a saying "the way to a man's heart is through his stomach." Notice that Mrs. Fanshawe has prepared an elaborate meal, on her best china, with salmon, asparagus, cheeses, and, as the narrator puts it, "the works." Oral pleasure, which is a form of sexual pleasure, becomes a prelude for genital sexual pleasure. Eating and drinking are, we must remember, often preludes to genital sexual pleasure. We are talking here about matters like taste and smell.

Smell

There is no indication of the power of smell in seduction in this scenario. Auster doesn't say whether Mrs. Fanshawe is wearing perfume, but we know that smell plays an important role in sexual behavior and other kinds of behavior, as well. In the lower animals, smell often indicates that a female is ready for sex and impregnation. With humans, we use artificial agents of smell, though there is some research to the effect that natural smells given off by males and females play a role in sexual behavior.

Drink.

The seductress has had a lot to drink and the narrator, her "victim" also has drunk a goodly amount of wine and is somewhat drunk. In such a state, it is fair to suggest, one's resistance is compromised. The narrator recognizes that he is drunk but says that drunkenness is not enough to lead to one's being seduced.

Talk.

One technique Mrs. Fanshawe uses to seduce the narrator is to talk to him and to spellbind him. He finds himself hypnotized by her talk and that nothing could touch him. He was "floating" inside her words, he tells us. Talk is very important for if seduction is seen as a kind of persuasion, the language that is used to seduce a man becomes of critical significance.

The narrator speaks of being enchanted by the "rise and fall of syllables" as Mrs. Fanshawe spoke.

Lighting

Generally speaking, we think of seductions as taking place at night and in dimly lit rooms, where a romantic atmosphere can facilitate the seduction. But there is no reason why a seduction can't take place in the afternoon. In any case, the quality of light has a role in seduction. The narrator is spellbound by the sparkle of the sunlight on the sauces and the radiance of the sun as it streams into the room.

Visual Images

Visual images are also important here. We have just seen how important the sunlight was. In many seductions, a woman wears revealing clothes—showing her cleavage, revealing various parts of her body, her legs, and so on—that stimulate sexual desire in men. In this case, we have an image of a partially naked beautiful woman, carried for many years in the seduced man's mind, of the woman who is seducing him. We are told, incidentally, that Mrs. Fanshawe, when she was young, was extraordinarily beautiful and that she is still a beautiful woman.

Memory

It is the memory of having seen a partially naked Mrs. Fanshawe that is at work here, not the way she is dressed while she is seducing the narrator. Quite likely, memory of beautiful women—in various stages of dress and undress—plays a role in seduction scenarios. It is in memory, after all, that our erotic fantasies linger.

Recognition

The narrator in this seduction scene realizes that Mrs. Fanshawe is attempting to seduce him. He tells himself, from time to time, to "watch out." But he is powerless to resist, having been hypnotized by her language. There seems to be a slow, subtle process by which his resistance is overcome and his knowledge that he is being seduced becomes irrelevant, as he is overwhelmed by passion and desire. At some moment, so this scenario suggests, the awareness a man has that he is being seduced and his fear about its consequences gives way to his passion and his desire for immediate sexual gratification.

This seduction scene also suggests the power of technique over reason. Mrs. Fanshawe is an older woman, still beautiful, but not sexually desirable by the narrator, who is married to a very beautiful young woman, Sophie. But Jane Fanshawe is able to outwit the author and seduce him, even though her reasons for doing so—and his—are both connected to darker forces in their psyches: her desire to be hurt and his desire to be cruel and to use her to attack Fanshawe.

Touch

It is touch, a physical connection between Mrs. Fanshawe and the narrator, that triggers the actual seduction. He has gone over to comfort her, as she sits crying. The moment he touches her, there is an electric spark that is generated, creating a memory of other bodies he had touched and other women he had embraced. This leads to the two of them kissing and having passionate sex together in her bedroom.

A Summary

There are, then, eight aspects to the Narrator's seduction by Mrs. Fanshawe in *The Locked Room*. These aspects—I don't want to say steps because they don't have to occur in any logical or predetermined way—offer, I would suggest, an anatomy of female seduction techniques. But at a very abstract level.

Societies differ in terms of what foods are served, what wines or other alcoholic beverages are consumed, what kinds of perfumes are used, what the conversation is like, and so on, during seductions. The devil, as they say, is in the details.

Part IV:

Screen Seductresses

CHAPTER 14

MARLENE DIETRICH: THE AMBIVALENCE OF SEDUCTION

Marlene Dietrich was born on Dec. 27, 1901 as Maria Magdalene Dietrich and while in her twenties found small roles in the theater and eventually a leading role in her first film, *Die Frau, Nach Der Man Sich Sehut.* Probably Dietrich's most famous role was as Lola Lola in Joseph von Sternberg's 1930 classic *The Blue Angel.* In *Mirror, Mirror: Images of Women Reflected in Popular Culture,* Kathryn Weibel describes their relationship: (1977:104, 105)

> In attempting to describe Garbo and Dietrich, critics have used words like "masculine" and "androgynous" in part because both actresses conveyed a highly charged, self-confident, and strangely self-sufficient sexuality....Ironically, Dietrich's demimonde image was molded by an American from Brooklyn, Joseph von Sternberg. (The "von" was an artificial acquisition; Dietrich called the director "Sternie.") In the late twenties Sternberg met Dietrich in Berlin, where she was an overweight, small-time actress. He reportedly ordered her to lose weight and began the indoctrination process whereby she was to learn the sizzling poses and gestures that made her famous. Dietrich made only seven films with Sternberg in the early thirties—including *The Blue Angel* (made in Germany), *Morocco, Dishonored, Shanghai Express, Blond Venus, the Scarlet Empress,* and *The Devil is a Woman*—but they created her legend.

For Weibel, Dietrich epitomizes "transcendent sexuality on the screen," and Dietrich did a wonderful job of maintaining and nurturing this brilliant illusion of herself for many years—from her film *The Blue Angel* until her death in 1992, at the age of 91. Her last cabaret performance was in 1974 and she made her last film, *Just a Gigolo,* in 1975.

In *The Blue Angel,* she seduces and then destroys (or perhaps "leads to destruction" is more apt) a straight-laced and tyrannical schoolmaster, Professor Rath. He is hated by his students and is portrayed as rigid and hateful. His room, spare and jail-like, reflects his constricted temperament. He is very proud of his position, which has a great deal of status. As he tells Lola, when he first meets her, "I am the master from the local school." To which she replies, "Then you should know enough to take off your hat."

Dietrich's gorgeous legs and those wonderful cheekbones are shown to great advantage by the lighting employed in the film. She exudes a sultry sexuality that is enhanced, actually, by the black and white film. The song she sings in the film, perhaps her most famous song, "Falling in Love Again," is worth examining in some detail.

"Falling In Love Again" Analysis

I will deal with some of the lyrics and their implied meanings in the first stanza of the song. I will only use some of the words in the lyrics in this analysis because of the difficulty involved in getting permission to use lyrics in songs:

....again.

The term "again" offers, perhaps, an ironic comment on the phrase "falling in love." The "again" suggests that she has fallen in love before—and given the looks of the singer, we are to assume many times. But it is the falling part, more than the love part, that is most significant here. The "falling" suggests, in the context of her image as a seductress, falling to the prone position to have sex rather than becoming involved in a strong emotional relationship. Falling also alludes to the fall in the Bible.

Never....

Here we see that this "falling in love" is something that happens independent of her wishes. She "never" wants to do this, but we are to assume she "often" does.

…Can't help….

This line reinforces her portrayal of herself as a "victim" of her emotions, of her inability to restrain herself from emotional and sexual relationships with men. If you wish to be cynical, the "falling in love" is really a means of putting a positive cast on her behavior and describing seduction as love. She tells us that she can't help herself and thus does not deserve any condemnation for her behavior.

…always my game.

The term "game" is worth considering here. Is love a game? If so, that means someone wins and someone loses in the game of love. There are rules to games that players must follow. Furthermore, in games people who play the games sometimes cheat. In addition, games end when people get bored with them. Love is her game, which suggests she has a certain amount of expertise in the game of love.

Play it…

In this phrase she alludes to the way in which she "plays" the game of love. There is a suggestion that she plays "love" to suit her needs and that she is not seriously involved with love.

Men cluster….

One reason she can play the game of love so well is that men are attracted to her. This implies that she has a certain kind of sexual appeal that makes her an object of male sexual desire. They "cluster" to her as if they need one another to gain support in the enterprise of getting her attention and getting her to "play the game of love" with them. A different reading of this line is that men are so enthralled with her that they don't care if there is a great deal of attention for her favors.

Like moths….

This simile suggests there is a kind of natural force to her sexuality that draws men to her the way moths are drawn to flames. There is also a suggestion of heat and sexual passion from the term "flame" and of danger. She hypnotizes and tantalizes, like a flame…and she also burns. We all have seen moths who can't keep away from flames, though these flames will destroy them if they get too close.

…I'm not to blame.

In this line the danger is spelled out. Like moths that burn their wings by getting too close to a flame, men set the stage for their own destruction by getting involved with her, but these men are incapable of resisting her overpowering sexuality. She, however, takes no blame for the self-destructive acts men do on her behalf when they get involved with her. She is innocent…at least in her own mind. "I know," she tells us, that she will not accept any blame for what men do because of her. She also is a creature controlled by natural—maybe even glandular forces— and cannot be held responsible for her behavior.

On Dietrich's Cross Dressing

There was a famous incident involving Dietrich that took place in Paris in 1933. Dietrich wore a jacket and pants and this led the chief of police in Paris to say that she would have to leave town if she continued to wear pants. She dealt with this by putting on a skirt, but wearing a man's hat, collar and tie. Her jacket was very tight and it emphasized her curves and sexuality. She has also worn men's clothing in her acts; her signature costume is a man's top hat and tails. In *Morocco* she plays a nightclub singer named Amy Jolly. In one famous scene, wearing her top hat and tails, she kisses a woman directly on the lips.

Male dress, on a woman, can have a number of different meanings. When Dietrich wears a top hat and tails, in one sense it is a means of showing how powerful her sexuality is, though at the same time it is a means of suggesting she has a hidden sexual identity. Dietrich was, it is widely believed, a bisexual who had many lesbian liaisons. A famous description of Dietrich is that "she is sexy but of indeterminate gender!"

It is worth noting that prostitutes often have appropriated men's clothes. As Ruth P. Rubinstein writes in *Dress Codes: Meanings and Messages in American Culture* (1995:108):

> In a chronicle describing the customs and habits of the people of Venice, Cesare Vecellio reported that by 1590 prostitutes had adopted elements of male dress as part of their seductive attire. Made of silk or other cloth, depending on the prostitute's social class, their "vests were padded and fringed in the style of young men, particularly Frenchmen."

As Rubinstein points out, before unisex became fashionable, when women wore men's clothing it called attention to them because it was unexpected and suggested a certain daring and perhaps even iconoclastic personality. It also often indicated homosexuality.

I would suggest, then, that Dietrich's "cross dressing" reflected her enormous confidence in her sexual identity and could be seen as something of a dare. "See," she says, "I'm such a powerful sexual figure that I can wear men's clothes and still be seen as a beautiful and seductive woman." Ironically, considering her film roles as a sexy seductress, in her real life the people she wanted to seduce most of the time, it seems, were women.

One of Dietrich's many roles was, by a curious coincidence, that of Empress Catherine the Great of Russia, the subject of an earlier discussion in this book. Dietrich, the film's Catherine, was a much more glamorous than the real Catherine, but she does not have the real Catherine's energy, intellectual brilliance, endurance as a sexual being, or passion for men. But, of course, who—if anyone—could match Catherine in these respects?

CHAPTER 15

MADONNA: THE SEDUCTRESS AS POSTMODERN PROVOCATEUR

Madonna is one of the more interesting performers of recent times, whose notorious use of her sexuality and religious identity has led to legions of young women imitating her and has raised many questions about sexuality, religion and gender. As Marjorie Garber notes in *Vested Interests: Cross-Dressing & Cultural Anxiety* (1993:211)

> Madonna, the pop figure who perhaps more than any other has read the temper of the times, artfully manipulates these categories in many of her music videos, whose conflation of religious and erotic themes has sometimes scandalized her critics. The resonances of her given name (in full, Madonna Louise Veronica Ciccone) and reminiscences of her own Catholic upbringing inflect the tone of songs like "Papa Don't Preach" and "Like a Prayer." In restaging the latter for her "Blond Ambition" tour Madonna…uncannily evoked Hasidic as well as Catholic images when she and her back-up singers, dressed in long black caftans, waved their hands above their heads as they danced in a "church" lit with votive candles.

It is Madonna's power to use style and her ambiguous sexuality to create herself as a unique and distinctive icon that is so interesting. She does this through fashion and through her ability to continually create and recreate herself, often with sensationalist aspects, in the best postmodern tradition.

Madonna as a Provocateur

She is a provocateur and tease who, among other things, plays with her identity and also is not averse to parody, suggesting a postmodern comic sensibility. Thus, she parodied Michael Jackson at one Music Video Awards show. Dressed in a double breasted suit and wearing white socks and glittering black men's shoes, she imitated many of Jackson's moves...and, of special significance...his characteristic move of squeezing his crotch. But what does it mean for a woman to squeeze a missing phallus?

Garber describes this scene as "empowered transvestitism" and suggests how complicated it is to know what it all meant. After all, we had a woman impersonating a male star who is notorious for his androgynous presence and highly mannered style of dancing.

According to Garber, when Madonna grabbed at her crotch, imitating Jackson, she was asserting her femininity. As she writes: (1993: 127)

> Why is it shocking when she grabs her crotch, repeating as she does a gesture familiar to anyone who has watched a two-year old male child reassuring himself of his intactness? Not because it is unseemly for a woman to do this...although it may be, to some people...but because what she is saying, in doing so, is: I'm not intact, he's not intact; I *am* intact, this is what intact is.

Garber describes this as *fetish envy*, rather than what Freud would say...namely that Madonna's act reflected her penis envy. Madonna's celebrated gesture is, or should be construed as, an answer to Freud's question "What do woman want?" The answer, of course, Freud would say, is a penis. Her gesture is connected a problem that perplexes society...how do we make sense of gender? Gender is, we are now told, socially constructed. And so, might I add, is Madonna...a socially constructed icon who reflects, among other things, contemporary anxiety about sexual identity.

Does Madonna Subvert the Male Gaze?

Her music video, *Material Girl* (1985) relates to the anxiety about identity in her young female fans. In the video she parodies a famous dance by Marilyn Monroe in *Gentlemen Prefer Blondes* (1953). This film deals with the search by women for wealthy husbands. In the film, most of the shots of women show women as they are viewed by men…that is, the shots are examples of what feminist writers call the "male gaze." In her video, Madonna allegedly subverts this male gaze by making viewers see the different kinds of gazes that are found in the film.

Jodi R. Cohen deals with Madonna in *Communication Criticism: Developing Your Critical Powers.* (Her discussion is based on the work of E. Ann Kaplan, who has offered a complex semiotic analysis of Madonna and the editing in her music videos.) Cohen writes (1998: 185,186):

The narrative in the video involves multiple Madonnas. The audience is aware of a "real" Madonna that made the video. The story she tells is about Madonna #1 who stages a performance within the narrative, as well as the character of Madonna #2 who is Madonna #1 performing within the narrative. Madonna #1 and #2 are shown in various settings: the stage, a film of a performance on the stage, backstage, a dressing room, and outside the studio. Because the video is based on a film, these characters also refer to the mythic character of Marilyn Monroe.

The framing and editing of shots in the video are often ambiguous and allow viewers to position themselves in a variety of gazes and roles. For instance, the video opens with a classic male gaze. There is a close-up of a director, and then shots of a film starring Madonna. Another close-up of the director "with an obsessed glazed look on his face: cements his desire for the woman in the film. The camera then cuts a shot of the director and another man sitting in front of the film starring Madonna. The camera moves into a close-up of Madonna's face, looking seductively at the camera…

The use of editing and shots in *Material Girl* allegedly reflects the mindset of the young adolescent, who feels unconnected with society, powerless and marginal. This would explain why Madonna's music videos exert such a powerful influence on young women, for the videos capture the anxiety and alienation felt by many of these women.

There are some critics, I should add, who question whether *Material Girl* is, in fact, a parody and argue that Madonna seems to believe what she is allegedly spoofing and exploits the male gaze, and female gaze, for her own purposes. That would explain why her video *Dress You Up* focuses almost exclusively on her body and shows her dancing and twisting. This would suggest that Madonna is a narcissist who really desires the voyeuristic gaze of all the young women (and the men) who idolize her and is not attacking the gaze but, instead, exploiting it.

Identity, Resistance and Commodification

Madonna discussed her strategy of subversion and adopting a sexual persona in *Interview* magazine:

> *Madonna:*…it was a private joke between my girlfriend and me, that we were floozies, because she used to get it from her mother all the time, too…
>
> *Interviewer:* So somewhere you did like the floozy look.
>
> *Madonna*: Only because we knew that our parents didn't like it. We thought it was fun. We got dressed to the nines. We got bras and stuffed them so our breasts were over-large and wore really tight sweaters…we were sweater girl floozies. We wore tons of lipstick and really badly applied makeup and huge beauty marks and did our hair up like Tammy Wynette.

In her article "Female Address in Music Video" (*Journal of Communication Inquiry,* Winter, 1987, Volume 11, Number 1) Lisa A.

Lewis comments on Madonna's visual style and sees connections between it and her earlier years: (p. 79)

> Madonna combines contradictory accoutrements of a feminine presentation the affected attitude of a cinematic vamp. Bleached blonde hair proudly displays its dark roots. Glamour eye make-up and lipstick create a look that is liked to Marilyn Monroe but a cocky demeanor exudes a self-assuredness and independence to counter the outdated naïve image. Skin-tight, lacy undergarments and crucifixes add up to a blasphemous, "bad girl" affectation, particularly in a woman who, we are told in the promotional press, hated the uniforms at her own Catholic school.

Madonna, who has made millions from her videos and films, generally presents herself as a seductive vamp, but she should also be seen as an icon of consumer culture for young women. In the best postmodern tradition, she mixes up the codes of glamour and fashion to create stylistic trends. Macy's, recognizing Madonna's power and distinctive style, created a Madonnaland" in 1985 that sold the sweaters, pants, and other items of clothing and jewelry associated with her. Macy's had a Madonna look-alike contest that had an overwhelming response from young women, who told reporters they wanted to be famous and that they wanted to be seen...that is, to become the object of the male gaze. In Madonna, we have an interesting combination of seductive sexuality and commodification that has moved from the realm of personal relationships (the seductress wants money) to that of being an important socio-cultural phenomenon (the image of the seductress is used to sell clothes, jewelry, perfume and so on).

As one biographer of Madonna put it, "Madonna is everywhere." She is not just an entertainer but, at the height of her popularity, has become a symbol, an icon. And she has continued to be an important figure in American popular music and film to this day. In 1998, for example, she won six awards for her videos at the MTV Video Awards show. As a *Billboard* magazine review of a recent album of hers begins, "Madonna continues to reinvent herself on the album *Ray of Life.*" That, it seems, is her genius…to identify the latest trends in pop culture and to continually recreate herself by connecting with them in her songs and videos.

APPENDIX: TEN SCHOLARLY POSITIONS ON THE SEDUCTRESS

In this chapter we look at the complexities involved in making sense of the seductress. What motivates her? How should we understand her? How do we explain her? Or can we make any generalizations about seductresses that are valid?

The Rashomon Phenomenon

In Akira Kurosawa's marvelous film *Rashomon*, we learn that different people see the same thing…what went on in a grove…in different ways. A man has been killed and his wife raped (or was it a seduction?) by a bandit, but the characters involved in this episode offer wildly different stories about what happened. The wife says that in a trance, caused by his hateful eyes, she killed her husband, stabbing him with her knife. But the husband tells a different story and says that broken hearted, he committed suicide, stabbing himself with her knife. The bandit says he killed the husband during a sword fight and a woodcutter, who observed everything, agrees with him, though he said both fighters were terrified. I would suggest we call this matter of having different perspectives on the same thing "The *Rashomon* Phenomenon."

What we learn from *Rashomon* is what we learn from trials: people who see something happen or are involved in something that happened often have different stories to tell about what happened. Think, for example, of people involved in a car crash and witnesses to that car crash. It's not unusual for people to disagree with one another about many different aspects of what happened.

In the same light, scholars in universities look upon things with different disciplinary perspectives…often disagreeing with one another about how to describe and explain a given phenomenon. Thus, it is not remarkable to find that scholars might disagree with one another about how to explain and interpret the significance of seductresses.

Imagine, then, if you will, a seminar room in which ten scholars are offering presentations on the seductress. This is what we might hear if we were to have a seat in the room.

1. A Psychoanalytic Interpretation of the Seductress

Using Freud's notions about the psyche, we may say that the seductress is essentially an id figure…a woman whose sexual drives and desires have overwhelmed both her ego and her super-ego. In his *New Introductory Lectures in Psychoanalysis,* Freud described the id as follows:

We can come nearer to the id with images, and call it chaos, a cauldron of seething excitement. We suppose that it is somewhere in direct contact with somatic processes, and takes over from them instinctual needs and gives them mental expression, but we cannot say in what substratum this contact is made. These instincts fill it with energy, but it has organization and no unified will, only an impulsion to obtain satisfaction for the instinctual needs, in accordance with the pleasure principle (quoted in Hinsie & Campbell, 1970, p. 372).

The seductress is essentially id dominated, but she also uses her ego functions…which involve how an individual relates to her environment, because seductresses have to convince those they seduce to sleep with them…or indulge in whatever other form of sexual behavior they desire. They do this by using what Freud called our defense mechanisms, such as rationalization and suppression to obtain the satisfactions they desire.

It is possible to make a distinction between a woman who, at one point in time, becomes overwhelmed by desire and seduces a man and predatory seductresses who make a habit of seducing men. In the latter case we have behavior that Freudians might describe as an example of repetition compulsion, the need to repeat earlier experiences and certain behaviors as a means of obtaining sexual gratification and warding off unconscious anxieties and fears.

2. A Marxist Interpretation of the Seductress

From a Marxist perspective, the seductress is a product of bourgeois beliefs and values and is found only in capitalist economies. In socialist societies, where the sexes are treated equal and where the motto is "from each according to his or her ability, to each according to his or her need," sexuality is not an instrument of repression of the masses the way it is in Capitalist societies.

Thus, there is no need for women to seduce men to obtain sexual gratification or anything else. Capitalist societies treat sexuality the way they treat everything else…as something to be held in scarcity so it can be sold at a high price.

In a sense, then, the seductress in bourgeois societies is, without recognizing what she is doing, fighting against class domination and the control of the proletariat by the ruling class. The attitudes toward sex found in bourgeois societies are, after all, the ideas of the ruling classes…which use sexuality as a means of distracting members of the proletariat from class-consciousness.

Sexual behavior, we must recognize, is ideologically conditioned. This means that seductresses are actually warriors on behalf the of the downtrodden and poor, who function to attack and help destroy the ideological chains that bind the proletariat and prevent it from obtaining class consciousness. Seductresses, then, must be seen as waging war on the ruling classes; their behavior should be seen as part of the class conflict that ultimately will lead to the ruin of the bourgeoisie.

When a communist society is finally achieved, there will be no more seductresses because sex will no longer be seen as a scarce commodity that is sold as part of a consumer culture. In the Communist sexual paradise, the seductress will have no role to play.

3. A Sociological Perspective on the Seductress

Sociology is concerned with institutions and with groups of people, unlike psychology, which focuses on individuals and their psyches. Sociologists would be use concepts such as anomie, deviance, role, status and function to understand seductresses and those involved with them. Seductresses are anomic (no-norms) in that they don't accept the norms and values of the societies in which they live and indulge in behavior that is generally held to be deviant…that is immoral if not, in some cases, illegal.

When we come to social roles, we find a number of different players with whom the seductress is involved: a seduced male, a seductress, the police, religious entities, and the families of the seductress and the seduced male.

The seductress often is involved with the police (who may think she is a prostitute), religious entities with whom she is in conflict, and her family and the family of the male she seduced…especially if the seducer and seduced male are both married.

Sociologists might also suggest that there is a continuum that can be made of different kinds of sexual behavior, from frigidity to nymphomania. This is shown below.

1_____100

Frigid   Repressed   Disinterested   Normal   Seductress   Obsessive   Nymphomaniac

Thus, we can see that there are different attitudes about sexuality, from a woman who is frigid to a woman who is a nymphomaniac. It is difficult, in some cases, to separate one kind of behavior from another; thus, there may be an element of obsessiveness in the behavior of the seductress.

4. A Semiotic Perspective on the Seductress

Semiotics is the science of signs…signs being understood as anything that can be used to stand for something else. Thus, words are signs, facial expressions are signs, clothes are signs, bodies are signs, body language is a sign…just about everything is a sign. For the semioticians, human beings are sign sending and sign interpreting creatures.

Thus, from a semiotic perspective, the seductress in her "classic pose" is a woman who shows, by her clothes, makeup, hairstyle, use of perfume, her jewelry, her body language, and so on, what she is. She also uses signs…words…to persuade men to have sex with her. For example, consider the description of the seductress in the *Zohar:*

her hair all arranged, red as a rose,
her face white and red
six trinkets dangling from her ears,
on her neck all the jewels of the East….
 her lips beautiful, red as a rose,
 sweet with all the sweetness of the world.
 she is dressed in purple,
adorned with forty adornments minus one.

We can see, then, that there is a visual "look" to the seductress that most people can recognize.

Ferdinand de Saussure, one of the founding fathers of semiotics, suggested that "concepts are purely differential and defined not by their positive content but negatively by their relations with the other terms of the system." (1966:117). Thus, nothing has meaning in itself; we make sense of concepts, essentially, by seeing what they aren't, setting up in our minds a binary opposition—in this case, the virgin and the seductress.

There are also, let me suggest, other "poses" a seductress might take that hide her nature. One of the central tenets of semiotics is that if signs can be used to tell the truth, they can be used. With this in mind, let me list several of these poses.

The Innocent Little Girl. Here we have a woman who takes an ironic pose and presents herself as being like an innocent little girl. She may speak in a high voice like a child, dress in miniskirts and wear "baby doll" clothes, and thus looks like the opposite of what she really is.

The Nurse-Mother. This woman takes the role of a nurturing mother figure who seeks out men who are looking for "mother figures" because they represent acceptance and function as a substitute mother in certain respects.

The Mannish-Sexy Woman. Probably the quintessential figure who represents a "mannish-sexy" woman would be Marlene Dietrich. She may dress in pantsuits, shirts and even ties, and posses certain masculine traits but she still exudes a sexiness.

The Intellectual Woman. This pose represents a disguise meant to entrap intellectuals and people who are interested in ideas. The intellectual seductress may be well educated, accomplished in the arts and a person who aside from her predatory sexual behavior, seems concerned with the life of the mind. And she may very well be, but that is as a means of finding a certain type of man to seduce.

My point is, that aside from what we might call the classical seductress look, described in some detail in *The Zohar* and the Bible, there are many other "looks" a seductress can use. It is also reasonable to suggest that many woman who adopt a "seductress" look are not seductresses, but merely women experimenting with fashion and posing as what they're not for any number of possible reasons.

5. A Feminist Perspective on the Seductress

Why is it that some feminists have taken Lilith, a seductress, as a heroine? There are, it must be said, many different myths and interpretations about Lilith, so we have to recognize that descriptions of her as someone who strangles little children is only one view of her. Feminists see contemporary societies as phallocentric, dominated by the male phallus that in subtle ways shape a society's institutions and values. They argue that societies are male dominated, that the roles given to women in popular culture and the elite arts are all shaped, though we may be unaware of this, by male sexuality and male power.

Thus, Lilith, who stands up to males and subverts male sexuality and uses phallic power for her own purposes, can be seen…from this perspective…as a heroine for feminists. She is active instead of accepting the traditional role of women in society, being passive. In this respect, consider what John Berger writes about the way women are portrayed in western painting in *Ways of Seeing:* (1977:47)

> ...*men act* and *women appear.* Men look at women. Women watch themselves being looked at. This determines not only most relations between men and women but also the relation of women to themselves. The surveyor of woman in herself is male: the surveyed female. Thus she turns herself into an object...and most particularly an object of vision: a sight.

It is the desire of feminists that the change from being objects...especially sexual objects...who are seen, to subjects, who act, that explains why Lilith is a heroine for many feminists.

6. A Postmodern Perspective on the Seductress

Next, we come to the postmodern perspective. There is a great deal of controversy about how to define postmodernism, about what postmodernism is and is not and about what impact postmodernism has had on contemporary society. One general concept that postmodernism is identified with argues that the most fundamental value systems and belief systems that used to guide our behavior are no longer valid. As a famous postmodernist thinker, Jean-Francois Lyotard has put it, postmodernism involves "incredulity toward metanarratives." These metanarratives are the systems of belief (law, religion, philosophy) that used to be widely accepted and which helped shape people's behavior.

This means that seduction loses its negative connotations and becomes nothing more than one form of sexual behavior not much different from other forms of consensual sexual behavior. It probably is incorrect to argue that postmodernism is essentially anarchistic, and that in postmodern societies, anything goes. But certainly postmodernism offers a much freer kind of society than modernist ones.

As Simon Frith has explained in his book *Sound Effects: Youth, Leisure and the Politics of Rock 'n 'Roll,* as early as the 1960's, young people believed that "sex was best experienced *outside* the restrictive sphere of marriage, with its distracting deceits of love and long-term commitment" (1981:240). As a result of the pill and advances in birth control, attitudes towards sex changed. Frith writes: (1981:241)

> Sex became just another form of leisure, and the ideology of leisure began to change. Free time was used increasingly impulsively, irrationally, unproductively, with reference to immediate gratification rather than to usefulness or respectability or sense of consequence. The expansion of sexual opportunity, in other words, occurred in the context of a new leisure stress on hedonism, and the result was that sex became an experience to be consumed, used up in the moment, like any other leisure good. Sex was now defined without reference to domestic ideology or romantic love, but it was still gender-bound: men were, by and large, the sexual consumers; women were, by and large, the sexual commodities, their charms laid out for customer approval in a never ending supply of magazines and films and "spreads."

As a song popular in recent years put it, when it comes to sex, and seduction, we have to ask "what has love got to do with it?" That is a very postmodern question!

7. A Biological Perspective on the Seductress: Seduction and the Human Sensorium

Human beings are, in the final analysis, animals and we share, with other mammals, certain behavioral practices. We have certain needs and desires that are, in part, physical in nature, even though we also have culture and civilization, which have profound effects on our sexual lives.

Recently I watched a nature program about monkeys in Japan. One scene showed a female monkey, in estrus, crying out to attract male monkeys to come and impregnate her. Her howls and cries attracted a number of male monkeys who took care of her needs. Male animals learn which females are in estrus by the smells they emit. In many cases the males fight with one another to determine who will mount the female and in some cases, a number of different males mount the female over a number of days...or whatever period the female is in heat.

It isn't so simple with human beings. But women do use a variety of techniques...many of which are described in this book...to attract men they like and, in many cases, seduce them. They don't howl like the female monkeys when they are in heat. But they have similar aims, in many cases.

And like the female monkeys, and many other animals, women take advantage of smell. In fact, the whole sensorium, all the senses which human beings have, are often employed by women to seduce men. The sensory stimuli that can be employed are as follows: Auditory (hearing), Olfactory (smell), Tactile (touch), Thermal (heat) and Visual (sight). Let me offer a slightly different list, based on the letters "S" and "T," as a mnemonic device to aid in remembering them.

Sight. We know how important visual cues are in communicating and, of particular interest here, the power a beautiful woman has to excite men. Our sense of sight it affected by things like facial expression, dilated pupils, body language, fashion, lighting, the ambience of the room in which a seduction is begun and the room in which it is brought to a successful conclusion. So visual phenomena play an important part in seduction.

A good example of this is found in the lyrics of the song "Some Enchanted Evening." In this song, love is generated when someone "sees a stranger" in a crowded room and immediately falls is love. Many love poems also dwell on sight and the love caused by looking at a beautiful woman. In the Bible, there is a record of one unsuccessful seduction attempt by a woman, and that is told in the story of Joseph. He is sold to Potiphar, an Egyptian, and made his personal attendant. Potiphar's wife sees him and desires him:

After a time, his master's wife cast her eyes upon Joseph
and said, "Lie with me;" But he refused....And much as she

coaxed Joseph day after day, he did not yield to her request
to lie beside her, to be with her.

Frustrated by Joseph's unwillingness to sleep with her, she tells her husband that Joseph had tried to seduce her. This leads to Potiphar having Joseph thrown in jail. Potiphar's wife was not a particularly subtle seductress and was unsuccessful. But her desire for Joseph was set in motion by her casting her eyes upon him. In the Old Testament, the time between seeing a desirable woman and sleeping with her is often quite brief. David sees Bathsheba, desires her, sends for her and sleeps with her...all in the space of a sentence or two.

Smell. Perfume is the artificial means that women use to excite men. Scientific research has shown that smell has a powerful triggering effect on the human brain. This has led to the development of aromatherapy. In recent years scientists have discovered that women give off subtle, barely distinguishable smells that indicate their state of sexual desire and have the power to excite men, even though neither the women nor the men recognize that this process is going on.

Many perfumes now have names that suggest their power...Obsession, Tabu (taboo) and so on, and others are given an identity as sexual turn-ons by the advertisements that are made for them. In Saul Bellow's story, "Something to Remember Me By," the youthful narrator of the story becomes excited by the smells coming from a naked woman's vagina as well as by seeing her naked.

Sound. There are several aspects of sound that need to be mentioned. First, music has an affect on our psyches. That is the principle behind Musak, the piped in music heard in department store elevators and various work sites. The rhythmic and melodic quality of music and in some cases, the lyrics people know to popular love songs, all can help generate a romantic ambience.

In addition, there is the power of language, of words, to entertain and excite a man. The seduction of a man has a powerful verbal component to it as well as a strong physical one. Seduction is, in one sense, a means of persuading a man to do something that he probably had not anticipated doing, and might not want to do or be afraid to do for any number of reasons. In the novel *The Locked Room,* discussed earlier, the narrator tells how he is swept away by the words of the women who is in the process of seducing him, and even though he is aware that he is in danger of succumbing to her, he seems powerless to escape her.

Taste. In any number of portrayals of seductions by women, we find that both the seductress and the seduced male drink wine (or in some cases hard liquor) and often have a meal together. A man's stomach is held to be the way to his heart, and there is something about having a fine meal together that creates a sense of well being and pleasure that can be utilized by the seductress.

One thing about having a fine meal, especially in one's apartment or house, is that there is privacy and the easy availability of the bedroom. If we look upon a seduction as theater, the seductress controls the lighting, the set (the ambience of the apartment), the dialogue and, when successful, the resolution of the drama.

Temperature. The human body responds to heat and the temperature of a room may help facilitate a feeling of well being and pleasure that is useful to the seductress. A warm, balmy day seems more conducive to sexual seduction than a cold one. In common language, we often talk about sexual desire in terms of heat..."all hot and bothered," and so on. And a woman's sexual receptiveness is often tied to temperature as when we describe a woman (like an animal) as being "in heat." Beautiful young women are commonly described now as "hot."

Touch. One way or another, the seductress must find a way to induce the man she is seducing to touch her. This touch often has an electric quality to it, leading to kissing and then sexual relations. Touch plays an important part in lovemaking and foreplay, also...since we use touch to stimulate the body's erogenous zones.

It is obvious, then, that seduction is a highly sensory matter and women who seduce men use the various senses to achieve their aims. We use the senses to talk about knowledge and ideas, also. Thus, for example, a person might say, "I see what you mean" suggesting the vision and sight are important ways of understanding ideas. Other people might say, "I hear you," indicating that they have heard what you said and understand the point you are trying to make. Still others talk about understanding in terms of feelings. They say things like "I feel this way about the matter" or "I feel your argument is correct," giving primacy to the sense of touch.

Our senses play an all-important role in our lives, though we seldom think about them unless we suffer some kind of a physical ailment that disturbs our sensorium. So it is only natural that seduction involves the senses and when it comes to seducing men, women can say "the more senses the better."

8. A Linguistic Perspective on the Seductress: Language, Sex and Seduction

In Theodore Thass-Thienemann's *The Interpretation of Language* Volume II: Understanding the Unconscious Meaning of Language (New York: Jason Aronson. 1973) we find a number of interesting thoughts about language and sexuality. For example, Thass-Thienemann points out that there is even a sexual dimension to the terms "bored" and "boring." That stems from the fact that the male sexual organ during an erection stands out from a man's body and is capable of "penetrating" a woman's vagina.

Fantasies women have about having sex with men, or actually having sex with men while too young, can lead to a deadening of a female's fantasy life and a sense that life is boring. As he writes (1973: 63, 64)

> It is essential for the proper understanding of these verbal instances that the female does not see her organs except in a mirror, while the organ of the male is *outstanding*. There are many

clinical illustrations of the French *main-tenant;* in dreams holding the male organ gives the dreamer the feeling of stark reality.

The early seduction of the female, as this has been observed, may result in arresting the luxuriant fantasies which flourished before the girl experienced the reality of the sexual encounter. Premature sexual stimulation may even lead to later frigidity, apathy, and boredom....the male is "boring" and the female the "bored" one.

In this passage we see that males take on their customary role of being active and females of being passive: men are boring, women are bored. The sexual connotations of these two terms must not be underestimated.

Thass-Thienemann continues his analysis with a discussion of the German terms for chaste and lewd: (1973:116)

The German noun *Zucht* and its adjective *zücht-ig* absorbed in the course of the Middle Ages all the high religious and moral qualities of chivalry, but *züchtig,* meaning "chaste," "modest," qualities the sexual connotation even in the modern language. This connotation becomes more apparent by its negative form: *Un-zucht* means "lewdness" and *un- züchtig,* "lewd, lascivious....."

The German language, it seems, uses a negation of a term with positive connotations to suggest a wanton character in a woman. Using the negation would suggest that the norm is chaste and modest behavior and behavior that is not zucht is, therefore, unusual or aberrant.

Finally we come to marriage from its linguistic aspects. Domestication is a term that can be applied to humans and to animals...like dogs and to a lesser degree cats. A strong woman must be "tamed"...a concept that Shakespeare used, to great advantage, in his comedy *The Taming of the Shrew.*

Women it is suggested are, by nature, wild and must be "tamed" in order to be turned into domesticated creatures. In Shakespeare's play, it turns out, all the shrew needed was to hear that she was loved to initiate a process of her eventually becoming "domesticated." Thass-Thienemann explores the roots of this idea in Greek, suggesting it is found in most Indo-European languages:

> The general English term for domestication is *to tame.* This is an old genuine term with phonetic parallels almost in all Indo-European languages. The according Greek verb is *damao* or *damadzo,* said of animals "to tame, break in, bring under the yoke," of maidens "to make subject to a husband," but in the passive "to be forced or seduced" or "to subdue of conquer." Thus in Greek the "wife" was called *damar,* properly "one that is tamed or yoked," whereas the maiden was *a-damastos,* "untamed." In German the act of seduction or rape is termed by the fantasy of "violently pulling," *Not-zucht,* which might be understood in these connections.

The seductress is the woman who has not been tamed and who refuses to be tamed. If she is married, and an adulteress, she pretends to have been domesticated, but that is only an act. In reality she is unyoked and thus she "pulls" men to her, using her beauty and her charms and all the other things the seductress has at her disposal.

Finally, there is a suggestion, based upon our language, that the Garden of Eden, as a Garden of Delight, is the proper home of the seductress. We learn from Thienemann that the term "delight" has two meanings: (1973:190)

> The shadow of bad conscience is conspicuous in the word *delight* (which is, in turn, from *de-lecto, are),* which means, on the one hand, "to delight, please, charm, amuse" and on the other "to allure from the right path, entice away, seduce." In the Biblical account we see the close association of *Eden,* meaning "delight" and the act of enticement: claiming to be seduced or enchanted relieves the self from a bad conscience and responsibility by projecting one's own guilt upon the source of the delightful gratification.

His notion that seduction is a kind of weasel-word that enables people…in our case, men…to enjoy the sexual act yet escape from having a sense of guilt about it, is worth serious consideration.

It raises the issue of the degree to which the seductress always has "unwilling" men to seduce, or, at least, the matter of how difficult it is to seduce men. The bad name the seductress has may be a convenient means for men to blame someone else for their moral shortcomings or their inability to control their physical appetites. Defining the seductress as irresistible, as a femme fatale, enables men to see themselves as victimized for having sex with a woman outside the bounds of marriage or overtly consensual sex.

9. An Ethical Perspective on the Seductress

Ethics is a very complicated subject. There are considerable disagreements among professional ethicists and among the general public, about what is and what is not ethical behavior. For example, some ethicists argue that behavior is relative to cultures. Thus "when in France, do as the French do." Other ethicists are absolutists and argue that certain behavior is wrong, even if it is considered acceptable in certain cultures or among certain groups. If there are standards of right behavior that should be applied to all people, that are absolute, how do we determine them?

We also make a distinction between laws and morals. One obeys laws for a variety of reasons, such as the fact that we can be punished for disobeying them. Moral behavior is a different matter. for it involves our evaluating possible actions and deciding which actions are good and which ones are evil. Just because something is legal doesn't mean it is moral; for example, once slavery was legal. But it was still immoral and thus someone who fought against slavery was acting morally, though perhaps illegally.

The Problem of Means and Ends

One commonly understood principle of ethics is that people should be used as "ends" not "means to an end." That is, we shouldn't *use* people for our own purposes. Thus, we should be friends with people because we like them, not because they can be helpful in getting a job or because they can be of use to us in some other manner. We should associate with people because we like who they are not what they can do for us.

This would suggest that women who seduce men (and vice versa) which involves "using" someone else for sexual gratification and possibly for other means, are acting in an unethical manner. They are not treating the men they seduce as "ends," but are using them for their own purposes: sexual gratification and perhaps something else as well.

In addition, there is the problem that arises when a woman seduces a male who is married or even engaged to someone else. A married man who is seduced by a woman becomes an adulterer…a man who is unfaithful to his wife (and his family) or his fiancée, if he is engaged. Thus, he violates the trust that has been placed in him and this, most ethicists would argue, is an example of immoral behavior.

But what about women like Judith, who seduces a man to save her people? Is this an ethical act?

The Problem of Judith

Judith, remember, seduces an Assyrian general, Holofernes, so she can save her people from destruction. He is overwhelmed by her beauty and loses any sense of restraint. He drinks too much so he becomes powerless. And then Judith cuts off his head. So we have in Judith a seductress and a murderess who has become a great heroine. How can we explain this?

The answer is that in beheading Holofernes Judith was saving the Jews from a tyrant who would have killed many people and destroyed the Temple. Thus, unless you consider killing to be wrong under any circumstances…that is, the commandment "Thou shall not kill" is an absolute

that must be followed in all cases. If this commandment is an absolute, we cannot protect ourselves against a person who attempts to kill us. What we do is use the notion that we shouldn't kill as a general rule of conduct, but recognize that it is right to kill in self-defense.

If killing Holofernes is considered to be a moral act, and can be construed as an act of self-defense, then using seduction as a means to obtain this end becomes a moral act as well. So seduction can, in certain circumstances, be recognized as a moral act. We can make the same point about women spies who seduced Japanese or German soldiers and military officers during the Second World War to obtain valuable information to aid us in our fight against the Axis powers.

There is, in much of our popular culture…especially in a number of films…a strong connection between seduction and killing, as vamps destroy the men they have seduced and their sisters in seduction, vampires, actually kill their victims. But this kind of killing is not moral.

One can, perhaps, argue that showing how dangerous seductresses are, so as to persuade men to avoid becoming involved with them, is a moral act on the part of the novelist or filmmaker. In many films, the consequence of seduction is death.

Technology and Seductresses

It is quite likely that women have become bolder in their sexual relationships due to new technological developments such as the birth control pill and intrauterine devices. They free women from the fear of becoming pregnant after having sex.

Thus, it is possible that now that women have gained the power to control contraception…a power that used to be controlled by men, through the use of condoms…they have felt more enabled to take the initiative and become seductresses. This would just be one more example of the power of technology to affect moral behavior.

In his book *Desexualization in American Life,* anthropologist Charles Winick has an amusing description of a fashion that was popular a number of years ago, the so-called "wet" look. As Winick writes (199 :317)

> We may speculate that one reason for the current success of women's dresses, coats, and boots of vinyl, in spite of the mater-

ial's stiffness and non-porousness, could be that a woman in vinyl somewhat resembles a penis sheathed in a condom.

Thus, our seductress, dressed in her vinyl dress, coat and boots, now resembles a penis in a condom. She thus functions as a "turn on" for men she wishes to seduce…reminding them that they could be putting on a condom to use with her.

It is possible to argue, then, that the behavior of seductresses if often morally ambiguous. Thus, a woman who seduces a man can, in certain circumstances, do so for moral reasons: to save her people, to prevent evil acts, or even to help the male who has been seduced. And also, there is the fact that the seductress while giving pleasure to herself also, at the same time, gives pleasure to the male who has been seduced.

So we have to be careful when we consider the moral aspects of seduction. They often are much more complicated than we might imagine and we do violence to things when we assume, automatically, that seductresses are always acting in an immoral nature.

10. A Pragmatist's Conclusion: The Consequences of Seduction

The consequences of seduction are often deleterious to the health and well being of the men who have been seduced. The following chart lists some of the most famous "victims" of seductresses and may help explain why many men harbor unconscious (and in some case conscious) fears and anxieties about seductresses, women, and sex, in general.

Seductress	Consequences for Seduced Male
Lilith	Seduced Adam…kills or harms children
Judith	Cut off Holoferenes' head
Delilah	Led to Samson being blinded, then killing himself
Salome	Had John the Baptist beheaded
Potiphar's Wife	Had Joseph thrown into jail for refusing her advances
Circe	Turned men into swine

Sirens Lured seafarers to their destruction
Monica Lewinsky Led to President Bill Clinton's impeachment
 Seductresses and Consequences for their Victims

The Vamp and the Virgin are the two polar extremes we can consider when talking about seductresses. In Bram Dijkstra's *Evil Sister: The Threat of Female Sexuality and the Cult of Manhood* (Knopf, 1966:12) we see the two polar extremes compared:

> Theda Bara's subsequent, oft-repeated and highly influential screen performances as a sexual predator soon also made "vamping" into a widely recognized verb for antisocial feminine behavior of a sexual nature. Thus her actions gave a generic name as well as a new profession the thousands of future cinematic vamps whose task it would be crawl through screendom in dualistic opposition to the ever diminishing ranks of virginal heroines styled after Lillian Gish and Mary Pickford. Cinematic vamps came to lord it in very unequal fashion over the "virgin" wives of the filmic bourgeois household. The angels of domestic mercy whose task it was to tend lovingly to an unending procession of straying husbands were effectively relegated to the periphery of most screenplays, to make way for a new category of female predators eager to lead civilized men of business astray. (p

Certain women, we see, are very dangerous and becoming involved with them leads, almost inevitably, to very bad consequences. And good women…virgins and wives…it seems are powerless to fight against the sexual allure of these vamps. Using Dijkstra's opposition between the vamp and the virgin as a starting point, let me offer a chart that shows the difference, in graphic detail, between these two archetypal figures.

The Vamp   **The Virgin**
Vampire   Virgin Mary

Seduces	Sanctified
Active Sexually	Passive Sexually
Sexual	Chaste
Demonic	Saintly
Satanic beauty	Godly beauty
Darkness	Light
Experience	Innocence
Desire	Love
Death of Victim	Salvation
Masculinized female	Desexualized female

The Vamp and the Virgin Compared

On the left, under the Vamp category, we have a picture of the seductress and her attributes and on the right, under the Virgin, the characteristics of the virgin and the consequences of her saintly role. These opposition are, perhaps, a bit simplistic and overdrawn, but they do suggest...in rather extreme ways...the difference between vamps and virgins.

There is some reason to suggest that seductresses are "masculinized" women in that they have taken on the pro-active role traditionally held by the male in sexual relationships. They are not physically masculinized, however. The virgin, to the degree that she abstains from sexual relationships, can be seen as a desexualized female, one who has abandoned sexual relationships in the name of a higher love.

The "good wife" is the virginal woman who fights with the vamp and generally is defeated in films and other works of pop culture, since the power of vampish sexuality is portrayed as too great for virginal (that is, saintly) love. Vamps (a shortened form of weaker version of vampires) are irresistible and destructive in the popular imagination. And so, it seems, are seductresses.

BIBLIOGRAPHY

Auster, Paul. *The Locked Room.* 1986. New York: Penguin Books.

Barthes, Roland. *A Lover's Discourse: Fragments.* (transl. Richard Howard). 1978. New York: Hill and Wang.

Brenner, Charles. *An Elementary Textbook of Psychoanalysis (Revised Edition).* 1974. New York: Anchor Books.

Dijkstra, Bram. *Evil Sisters: The Threat of Female Sexuality and the Cult of Manhood.* 1996. New York: Alfred A. Knopf.

Durant, Will. *Caesar and Christ.* 1944. New York: Simon and Schuster.

Fast, Julius. *Body Language.* 1971. New York: Pocket Books.

Freud, Sigmund. (Joan Riviere, transl.) *A General Introduction to Psychoanalysis.* 1961. New York: Washington Square Press.

Girard, René. *Deceit, Desire & the Novel: Self and Other in Literary Structure.* 1965. Baltimore, MD: Johns Hopkins University Press.

Graves, Robert and Patai, Raphael. *Hebrew Myths: The Book of Genesis.* New York: McGraw-Hill.

Huizinga. J. *The Waning of the Middle Ages.* Undated. (transl. F. Hopman). New York: Doubleday Anchor Books.

Matt, Daniel. *The Essential Kabbalah: The Heart of Jewish Mysticism.* 1996. San Francisco: HarperCollins.

Musil, Robert. *The Man Without Qualities.* Volume 1. (Eithne Wilkins & Ernst Kaiser, transl.) 1965. New York: Capricorn Books.

Ovid. *The Love Poems.* (transl. A.D. Melville). 1990. New York: Oxford University Press.

Ovid. *The Art of Love.* (transl. Henry T. Riley). 1949. New York: Stravon Publishers.

Patai, Raphael. *Myth and Modern Man.* 1972. Englewood Cliffs, NJ: Prentice-Hall

Rubinstein, Ruth P. *Dress Codes: Meanings and Messages in American Culture.* 1995. Boulder, CO: Westview Press.

Spillane, Mickey. *I., The Jury.* 1947. New York: New American Library.

Tanizaki, Junichiro. *Naomi.* (transl. Anthony H. Chambers). 19 New York: Alfred Knopf.

Thass-Thienemann. *The Interpretation of Language: Volume II: Understanding the Unconscious Meaning of Language.* 1973. New York: Jason Aronson.

Ustinov, Peter. *Five Plays.* 1964. Boston: Atlantic Monthly Press.

Winick, Charles. 1995. *Desexualization in American Life.* New Brunswick, NJ: Transaction Books.

ABOUT THE AUTHOR

Arthur Asa Berger is professor of Broadcast and Electronic Communication Arts at San Francisco State University, where he has taught since 1965. He graduated in 1954 from the University of Massachusetts, where he majored in literature and philosophy. He received an MA degree in journalism and creative writing from the University of Iowa, in 1956. He was drafted shortly after graduating from Iowa and served in the US Army in the Military District of Washington in Washington DC, where he was a feature writer and speech writer in the District's Public Information Office. He also wrote high school sports for *The Washington Post* on weekend evenings.

Berger spent a year touring Europe after he got out of the Army and then went to the University of Minnesota, where he received a Ph.D. in American Studies in 1965. He wrote his dissertation on the comic strip *Li'l Abner*. In 1963-64, he had a Fulbright to Italy and taught at the University of Milan. He also spent a year as visiting professor at the Annenberg School for Communication at The University of Southern

California, in Los Angeles in 1984 and was a Fulbright Senior Specialist professor at Heinrich Heine University in Dusseldorf in 2002.

He is the author of numerous articles, book reviews, and more than 40 books on the mass media, popular culture, humor, and everyday life. Among his textbooks are *Media Analysis Techniques, Media and Communication Research Methods, the Art of Comedy Writing*, and *Video Games: A Popular Culture Phenomenon*. He has also written a number of mysteries: *Die Laughing, The Hamlet Case, Postmortem for a Postmodernist, The Mass Comm Murders: Five Media Theorists Self-Destruct*, and *Durkheim is Dead* (in press). His books have been translated into German, Swedish, Italian, Korean, Indonesian and Chinese. He has lectured in more than a dozen countries in the course of his career.

Berger is married, has two children and one grandchild, and lives in Mill Valley, California. His wife teaches philosophy at Diablo Valley College. He enjoys travel and dining in ethnic restaurants.

He can be reached by e-mail at: aberger@sfsu.edu.

0-595-23077-6